SCOTTISH
DATES

Martin Horan

Chambers

Published 1990 by W & R Chambers Ltd,
43-45 Annandale Street, Edinburgh EH7 4AZ

British Library Cataloguing in Publication Data

Horan, Martin
  Scottish dates.—(Chambers mini guides series).
  1. Scotland, history
  I. Title
  941.1

  ISBN 0-550-20057-6

Illustrations by Julie Horan
Cover design by John Marshall

Typeset by Bookworm Typesetting Ltd, Edinburgh
Printed in Singapore by
Singapore National Printers Ltd

Preface

Scottish Dates is a pocket-sized look at Scottish history that everyone should find at once informative and enjoyable. It is more than the usual list of important historical dates covering kings and queens and battles, for it also contains information on a wide diversity of subjects from sport and entertainment to politics and literature.

It is essentially a book of interesting snippets; a kaleidoscope of facts pertaining to the development of the Scottish nation. So you will find out when Mary Queen of Scots had her head chopped off (1587) as well as the publication date of Sir Walter Scott's *Waverley* (1814), when the Forth Rail Bridge was opened (1890) and when the largest soccer crowd ever recorded in Britain watched Scotland play England (1937).

In this way **Scottish Dates** brings together the momentous and the anecdotal events of Scotland's past. A stimulating browse, a quick reference, a rewarding read, the book will be invaluable to all who enjoy reading a book about Scotland and the Scots.

Scottish Dates

80

Although the Romans had, under Julius Caesar, invaded
England in 55 BC, bringing it under their control and
reducing it to a province, they did not invade Scotland
until nearly a century and a half later.

In AD 80 Julius Agricola, Roman governor of the
province, crossed the Clyde leading an army into Scotland. He advanced slowly, building forts in advantageous positions, slaying warring bands from disunited
tribes called Britons. These were Cymric Celts whose
states called Cumbria or Strathclyde extended from
Lancashire to the Clyde. Their chief seat was at Alcluyd
or Dumbarton.

82

According to the historian Tacitus, Agricola's son-in-
law, the governor invaded Scotland, then called Alba
by its natives, during the reign of Domitan. Tacitus does
not, however, tell us whether the invasion took place on
the west or the east of the country.

83

Agricola crossed the Forth with a fleet complete with
land forces including cavalry. His crack fighters, the
9th legion, were wiped out by the Caledonians under
the cover of darkness while they slept. But the Caledonians were soon after made to flee and 'if the woods
and marshes had not favoured their escape, the single
action had put an end to the war.'

84

'Upwards of 30 000 men appeared in arms and their
force was increasing every day.' No longer were the Picts
and Britons disunited guerrilla bands. They were now
one unit under the great Caledonian chief Calgacus. He
is the first Scottish inhabitant to have a recorded identity,
if his name was not merely an invention of Tacitus.

Calgacus met Agricola at Mons Graupius. Tacitus records his famous speech to his troops before their meeting '. . . They made a solitude and they call it peace.'

It is claimed that no-one knows where Mons Graupius actually was though the 16th-century historian Hector Boece misspelt the name of the battle as Mons Grampians and the Grampian Hills were named after this literary error. Some early historians claimed it was on the moor of Ardoch and there is an Ardoch at the foot of the Grampians.

The Caledonians suffered a great defeat and Calgacus was among the fallen. There were 10 000 Caledonians slain compared to 340 Romans. For some time afterwards the land appeared to be completely deserted by the natives. Even the Roman scouts could not find any sign of life.

120

Emperor Hadrian, as a base for military operations against the north, 'fortified a line of about 80 miles from the Tyne, below Newcastle, to Bowness on the Solway'. The wall was about nine feet thick and eighteen feet high. On its north side was a ditch ten to twelve feet deep. To the south was an earthen rampart, a second ditch, then two smaller earthen ramparts. There were towers at intervals of a mile and about 20 well-fortified barracks or stations spread out the length of the wall. The construction of 'Hadrian's Wall' reveals the Romans' view of the northerners as hostile and dangerous.

139

Lollius Ubricus constructed a wall with about 20 forts from near Blackness on the Forth to West Kilpatrick on the Clyde. The wall was under the rule of Emperor Antonius Pius and though the land between the two walls was more or less subject to Rome, like Hadrian's Wall, Antonine's was often furiously attacked. The forts were lost and retaken on and off by the 2nd, 6th and 20th legions who held it 'during the 40 years of its existence'.

208

Lucius Septimus Severus, the Roman Emperor at this time, provoked by a general uprising of Caledonians, was determined to complete the conquest of the whole island of Britain. He never set eyes on the enemy because the Caledonians used guerilla tactics: attacking detached parties and cutting off stragglers. More than 50 000 Romans perished by these tactics and other hardships until Severus decided the land was not worth holding.

296

We find the first mention of the Picts at this time. They held the east of Scotland, north of the Firth of Forth. They left no literature and we do not know whether the word Pict is from the Latin *Picti*, meaning 'painted' – as the Romans say they were – or from the Latin word *Pehta*, derived from a Celtic word that means 'fighter' as they certainly were.

Many scholars have tried to prove they were Teutons while others have tried to prove they were Celts. It has been reckoned though that a continued stream of immigrants to Pictland (or Alba) made the Picts more Saxon that Celtic 'without changing the name of the state or dispossessing the leading families'.

360

The Scots are first mentioned at this time as one of the tribes fighting against the Romans in Britain. They did not use this name themselves. Latin writers had for a long time called the Irish this name (Pagan and Christian alike). These Irish were later to call their colonies in the Western Isles and Argyll by the same name. Their name – supposedly to have come from Scioth or Sythian, meaning wanderers – could have come from Heber Scott, a Hebrew king in Gallica (hence Gael) who was the father of Boamhain, first of the ancient Irish (Scots) kings.

They sided with the Picts against the Britons and, eight years later, with the Picts and the Saxons in an attack on the Romans in London.

368

Rome may have given Britain roads and buildings and peace but its influence never went much further than Roman settlements and was virtually non-existent in Scotland, where they achieved nothing more than a military occupation. This was the year when the Roman

Empire was split under Valentinian in the west and Valens in the east. Picts and Scots united, aided by Saxons, to harass them in the south of England. The Romans had allies among the Britons of the south but were defeated in London by the Picts, Scots and Saxons who plundered their riches.

432

The first great name connected with Christianity, irrespective of all theories as to how it was introduced, is that of St Ninian. He was also known as Ringan, Rinian and Trinian and said to be of royal birth and a native of Northumbria. He founded a church or religious house at Whithorn in Wigtownshire, Galloway. While there he tried to convert the southern Picts before preaching to the Picts of Perthshire. He had success with both groups. The little that is known of him and his missionary work is that it was early in the fifth century.

He died in *432*, the year when St Patrick went to Ireland. Patrick, said to have been born near Kirkpatrick on the Clyde, was not the first missionary there but is said to have been the most effective. As he is reckoned to have been a Romanised Briton it was probably the Roman – as opposed to Celtic – Christianity that he took there. Celtic Christianity flourished in Britain long before the Roman.

503

The Scots left Ireland, settled in Argyll where they built their state of Dalriada. They did so under Loarne More, their first leader of great fame, and brother of the High King Fergus MacErc.

506

Fergus is said to have brought 'lia-fàil' – the 'Stone of Destiny' – to Scotland. Some have claimed it was taken by another Fergus at a much earlier date.

According to Geoffrey Keating, the Irish-Gaelic historian (1570–1646), 'The Scots' [Irish Gaels] 'being persuaded that this stone possessed such power that Fergus the Great, son of Earc, having subdued the kingdom of Scotland and being determined to have himself proclaimed king sent an Embassy to his brother, Murtagh, son of Earc, requesting him to send him this

4

Stone, that he might sit upon it at the time of his Inauguration.'

However, Keating's history is not accurate — he maintained that the Picts were 'sent out' of the Irish province to settle in Scotland in the reign of Fergus. Presumably, he meant Fergus I who ruled Ulster (circa 330–305 BC). He, according to what early Scots believed, brought the Stone of Destiny to Scotland. He is credited with being the first to try setting up a dynasty in Scotland and may often have sailed back and forth between Ulster and Argyll.

Fergus the Great, or MacErc, died in 506.

563

The great missionary Columba, or Colum Cille, involved in civil strifes of Ireland, sailed for Iona and founded the celebrated monastery there. Of royal blood, he was closely related to several of the great Irish and Argyll Scottish families. His monastery, as the custom then was, was merely a wattled building or a 'creel house'. But it became a centre and a school from which monastery-founding missionaries were sent, not only all over Scotland and Northumbria, but also to France, Germany, Switzerland and Italy. Iona exercised authority over all the British monasteries and did not acknowledge the supremacy of the Roman Church.

637

The Scots power had grown and extended into Pictland. Though they still had connections with Ireland, the real power was in Argyll and so the Dalriada Scots attempted a conquest of Ireland. However, they were defeated at the Battle of Magh Rath, now Moyra, in County Down.

685

The Saxons of Northumbria were defeated by the Picts at Dunnichen (otherwise known as the Battle of Nechtansmere), which was probably in Forfarshire, and their King, Egfrid, was slain. It ended their ecclesiastical and political dominion over northern Britain. The Pictish King, Nechtan, rejected the Celtic Church and became a follower of the Roman one instead.

716

By this time the Celtic Church was no longer recognisable as such. This was the year when it conformed totally to the Roman doctrines and rituals.

733

Acca, Bishop of Hexam, a collector of relics, has been credited with bringing those of St Andrew to Fife, circa 733 and founding what has since become the town of St Andrews. There already was an ecclesiastical centre there. Some early writings say it was founded by an assistant of Columba, an Irishman called Rule or Regulus, circa 581–597. Another legend has it that the earliest ecclesiastical centre there was built by the Pictish King, Ungus, who reigned from 731 to 761.

826

The Church in Scotland moved its headquarters from Iona to Dunkeld because of the island's vulnerability to Norse attacks; the Norsemen were not averse to raiding churches.

843

Kenneth MacAlpin, otherwise known as Kenneth the Hardy, son of the Scots King and a Pictish princess, became the first King of both the Scots and the Picts, uniting the two nations.

937

The 'considerable imperialist' Athelstane, King of the Saxons and eventually of all England (and perhaps the first English King to claim sovereignty over Scotland), defeated a strong alliance of Irish and Northumbrian Danes and Strathclyde Britons at the Battle of Brananburgh. It took place on a 1000-foot flat-topped hill near the Solway. The *Anglo Saxon Chronicle* tells us it was the greatest slaughter in Britain until that time and that Constantine 'returned to the north in hasty flight'. This was Constantine II, the seventh King of the Scots after Kenneth MacAlpin.

943

After a period of about six years as Athelstane's vassal, Constantine II could put up with the indignity no longer. He resigned his throne to his cousin, Malcolm I, and returned to monastic life in St Andrews. Malcolm was crowned at Scone.

945

Malcolm I, 'a valiant prince and a good justicer', received the lease of the lands of Strathclyde on both sides of the Solway, probably from Edmund the Elder, the half-brother of Athelstane, who was crowned King of England in *940*.

The lease was not without condition: he had to become England's vassal. He accepted and, in case the lords of Strathclyde did not proffer their acceptance, Edmund put their lands to fire and sword to persuade them.

990

Kenneth III's army fought the Danes at the Battle of Luncarty near Perth. Legend has it that when the Danes sneaked up on the sleeping Scots camp – barefooted to prevent the sound of their approach – they unwittingly walked into a field of thistles. They cried out as the thistles stung, awakening the Scots who were roused into battle and who consequently routed the Danes. The same legend has it that from that time the Scots took the thistle as their national emblem.

1014

Malcolm II, Kenneth's successor after he slew him in *1005*, also defeated the Danes. He decimated their army in Mortlach, in Banffshire.

1018

Malcolm II, after being defeated by the Saxons at Durham, gained a victory over them at Carham. The very last mention of a Strathclyde prince is as an ally, or tributary, of Malcolm in this year.

1034

Malcolm II was slain by his successor and grandson, Duncan.

1040

Duncan was slain by *his* successor, MacBeth. Ironically, MacBeth's reign seems to have been more peaceful and stable than that of other kings of his time – although Shakespeare paints a different picture.

1057

Shakespeare's account varies considerably with historical detail. MacBeth was slain – but nowhere near either Birnam Wood or Dunsinane, though he suffered a defeat at Dunsinane. He met his end at Lumphanan in Aberdeenshire during an assault of Malcolm Canmore's troops and *not* at the hands of MacDuff. Malcolm was aided by the English King, Edward the Confessor, and by Siward, Earl of Northumbria. Malcolm was crowned as Malcolm III.

1068

The defeat and death of Harold II, King of the Saxons, two years previously at Hastings under William the Conqueror, drove many Anglo-Saxons to settle in Scotland. Among them came Edgar Atheling, heir to the Saxon throne, with his mother, two sisters and a band of loyal nobles. His sister, Margaret, married Malcolm and he in turn aided Edgar against William.

1093

Wars between the Normans in England and the Scottish-Saxon alliance continued for 25 years until Malcolm III led an army into England six years after William's death. He was, however, slain with his son and intended successor at Alnwick, though his younger son Edgar escaped. He fled to Edinburgh to tell his mother the bad news. She died of either shock or grief, or, indeed, of both.

1097

Edgar was placed on the throne after a four-year period of rule, or guardianship, of the country under Donald Bane, Malcolm's brother. Donald was co-ruler or guardian with Malcolm's illegitimate son, Duncan.

1107

Alexander I succeeded his brother Edgar as King. Their younger brother, David, at Edgar's bequest, was made ruler of Cumberland. Alexander soon 'carried forward the work of changing the Culdee for the Roman forms, and erected the bishopric of St Andrews'. It was consecrated by the Archbishop of York but his claim of supremacy over the St Andrews diocese was firmly rejected by Alexander.

1111

Alexander I, though a staunch upholder of Scottish independence from England, assisted the English King Henry I against the Welsh. The alliance probably happened because of the relationship of the two kings: Henry was not only his brother-in-law (through marrying Alexander's sister) but his father-in-law also, since Alexander was married to Henry's daughter Sibyl.

1120

Alexander I's reign had been peaceful until this year. Moray and Mearns lands, old Northern Pictavia, which 'had never greatly loved the descendants of Alpin', rose up against him. He was attacked in his favourite residence at Invergowrie but, having been forewarned, he was ready and drove his defeated enemies across the Moray Firth. It was Alexander's only war in Scotland.

1124

About two years after his wife died and was buried on an island in Loch Tay, Alexander I died on *23 April* at Stirling. His body was taken to Dunfermline where he was buried beside his parents at the Abbey of the Holy Trinity.

His brother David was crowned King. He had been a rich English noble, the Earl of Huntingdon. It is not clear whether the earldom was part of the inheritance of his wife, Matilda, heiress of Waltheof of Northumberland, or whether he had received it as compensation for Northumberland itself, that the King of England could not reckon as his own and would not like to see held by one who was already Prince of Cumbria and likely to become King of Scotland.

1135

David I had spent much of his time in England. Not only was his wife a great heiress there but his son had married into the family of Warrene and Surrey and his sister was Henry's Queen. She appointed her daughter Maud as successor to the English throne and ordered the English barons to swear allegiance to her.

On Edward's death in 1135 Stephen of Blois usurped the throne, backed by the Normans who were now firmly fixed in England. David marched with an army into Durham to assert Maud's claim. However, when he met Stephen, neither ventured into battle and the claim to Northumberland was left open. Other English fiefs, or lands held in fee, were given to David's son, Henry.

1138

David I led another army into England. He was met by a body of Normans at Northallerton. Their standard emblem was a wagon with a mast, itself bearing religious standards 'with the consecrated host at the top of all'. The idea of this car seems to have been taken from the great standard of car which was used by the people of Lombardy.

The Scottish army numbered 26000 but were 'ill compacted'. There were 'Lowlanders with cuirasses and long spears; men of Galloway with pikes only; men of Orkney and the Isles with their battle-axes; and Highlanders with their swords and small round shields'. Each attack they made was repelled and when a cry went up that David was slain there was further confusion.

Though baffled, David was not totally defeated at this 'Battle of the Standard'. He rallied his men and they wasted the English borders until Stephen gave up Northumbria. The rest of his reign was peaceful and it was during those years that he founded the abbeys of Holyrood, Melrose, Dryburgh, Kelso, Jedburgh, Newbattle and Kinloss.

1174

William the Lyon, David's grandson, was next on the Scottish throne and a year later he invaded Northumberland because Henry refused to restore it to him. Some Yorkshire barons made a hasty night march from Newcastle and, as they proceeded through a morning mist at Alnwick, saw a small group of horsemen practising lancing in a meadow. William, probably taking the barons for allies or friends, somewhat impetuously dashed towards them. He was immediately captured and taken to Henry at Northampton. From there he was conveyed to Falaise in Normandy, and only released on promise of doing liege homage for Scotland as Henry's vassal.

1176

On *9 August*, according to *Wynton's Chronicle*, 'in the presence of King William, two Scots bishops, and a brilliant throng of nobles and ecclesiastics, the grassy heights to the north of Brothock stream were solemnly consecrated.' This was the site of Arbroath Abbey that William had founded in memory of his friend Thomas A'Becket who was murdered eight years previously.

1189

After 15 years of liege homage, William the Lyon was at last released from his promise — but at a price. Richard the Lionheart acceded to the English throne that year and, intent on going to the crusades, he needed funds. To get them he offered to withdraw the conditions his father enforced on William — for 10 000 merks. William accepted and, in effect, Scotland's independence was restored.

1214

William the Lyon died in Stirling and his son Alexander II ascended the throne. The English barons were willing to accept his claim regarding Northumbria on condition that he aided them in their dispute with their King, John — who died two years later to be succeeded by his son, Henry III.

1239

Early in the 13th century, Gilbert, Bishop of Brechin, granted a charter to the Abbot and Monks of Lindores to establish schools in Dundee. It was confirmed by Pope Gregory XI on *14 February*.

1244

Though the Scots King held lands in Cumberland and Northumberland, these counties were largely English. Commissioners of both kingdoms could not agree as to the exact marches; the border line was much as it is today. Eventually two great armies met at the borders but though war had been threatening for some time, no fighting took place. Much of the old emnity had died out between the two sides – no doubt it had much to do with the fact that many powerful Norman families had arisen in Scotland with equal lands and connections in both countries.

1249

Alexander II had many difficulties among his Gaelic-speaking subjects – the main one being that they did not recognise themselves as his subjects! He had to deal with such people in the north, the west, and in Galloway. He set out on an expedition to the Hebrides to wrest these isles from the control of Norway. But he did not reach them. He died of a fever in his galley when it was anchored off the island of Kerrera, near Oban. He was 55 years old.

1251

The ten-year-old King Alexander III was married to Margaret, daughter of Henry III, at York. There he did homage for his Lordships of Penrith and Tyndale to acknowledge their feudal superiority. When asked to do homage for Scotland he replied, with a wisdom not likely to be his own, that it was a matter on which he had not as yet taken any counsel and was, besides, too important to be discussed at a marriage feast. This took place on *25 December*.

1263

Haco, King of Norway, was holding the Western Isles and the Isle of Man, the latter ruled by his son-in-law Magnus. Alexander set out on an expedition to win them back, and managed to get the allegiance of those chiefs who hated him less than they hated Haco.

Around the middle of *August*, Haco's fleet rounded the Mull of Kintyre and sailed into the Firth of Clyde. Although Alexander was a young man of 22 and Haco a veteran of 64, the younger man outwitted the older. He kept sending embassies of barefooted friars to Haco's flagship to sue for terms of peace. All the while he was stalling for stormy autumn weather, the depletion of the Norwegians' provisions and the recoupment of a Scottish force that was assembling in great numbers on the shore.

The night of *30 September* brought a storm so fierce and so sudden that the Norwegians believed it to have been raised by the spells of Scottish witches. The ships were ripped from their anchorage to be dashed against each other or run ashore in the pitch darkness. The terrified King ordered his priests into a boat and braved the enormous waves with them to the island of Cumbrae where a mass was performed. Unluckily for Haco it had no effect and the storm raged on all night and the next day. It scattered the Clyde with wreckage and the shore with stranded ships; the latter were attacked by armed peasants.

On *1 October* a large Scottish army furiously attacked the Norwegians on the shore at Largs. The Norwegians eventually got some backing from a couple of ships that managed to get to their aid with fresh troops. But after nightfall the weary Norwegians fled to their ships. Haco had to ask for a truce to bury his dead. He left with the tattered remains of his once magnificent fleet, sailing round the isles which were now lost to Norway forever. One night, when they reached Orkney, he ordered the chronicles of his ancestors, the pirate kings, to be read to him. Around midnight, as they were being recited, he died.

1272

Edward I, nicknamed Longshanks, succeeded his weak father, Henry III, as the King of England. Alexander gave homage at Westminster for the lands he held under Edward but when the Bishop of Norwich suggested that Edward should receive homage for Scotland, Alexander refused. He boldly stated: 'To homage for my kingdom of Scotland, none only but God had right; nor do I hold it of any but God alone.' This was a brave, if not rash, statement to make in front of the tyrannical King, also known as 'the Hammer of the Scots', on his own territory and surrounded by his own nobles.

1275

Work began on Sweetheart Abbey six years after the death of John Balliol (father of the John Balliol known as 'Toom Tabard' in Bruce's day) at the instigation of his wife. Devorgilla, who married Balliol when she was 19, funded the building of the abbey in her husband's memory. She also wanted it to stand as a monument to their love, thus the name Sweetheart Abbey. This was not its original name; it was also called Dulcecord. Its real name is New Abbey, to distinguish it from the earlier foundation of Dundrennan Abbey. Devorgilla, the daughter of Allan, Lord of Galloway, was also buried in the abbey next to her beloved husband. Her story is one of the great factual historical romances. The ruins of Sweetheart Abbey stand about six miles from the town of Dumfries.

1286

Alexander III's reign was relatively peaceful – and prosperous – according to the famous poem that tells us of the state the nation fell into after his death:

Sen Alexander our King wes deid
    That Scotland left in lufe and lee,
Away wes sonse of aill and breid,
    Of wine and wax, of gamin and glee.
The gold wes changit all in leid,
    The fruit failyeit on everilk tree.
Christ succour Scotland and remeid
    That stad is in perplexitie.

He died suddenly on the night of *12 March*. Alexander was riding in great haste to be with his wife, whom he loved dearly, when his horse stumbled. Both Alexander and the horse fell off the cliffs in Kinghorn, Fife, and plunged into the River Forth below.

1289

The Estates, who ruled along with the King, met at Scone and appointed six guardians over Scotland – a bishop and two barons for each side of the Forth. Edward did not demand guardianship; all he sought was the marriage of his son Edward to the young Queen, Alexander's daughter Margaret. The Scots were happy with the idea as the great families who were related to the royal house were more Norman than Scots. It was generally accepted that there would not be any more oppression – and a great deal less contention – with Edward as father-in-law to the Queen, than if control of her power and person was fought for by Norman families who were almost equal in power. The Scottish parliament proposed the marriage of Margaret, 'the Maid of Norway', with Edward's son. A marriage treaty, the Treaty of Brigham, provided that 'Scotland was to be kept a realm separate from England; its rights, laws, and liberties were to remain entire and inviolate; no crown vassal was to go forth of Scotland to do homage to a sovereign residing in England; no Scot was to answer beyond the marches in a civil cause or for a crime done in Scotland; and the great seal was always to be beheld by a native.'

1291

Margaret died the year before in Orkney and her death brought about 13 claimants to the throne. In *June* Edward I held a great meeting in Norham Castle on the Tweed, asking the pretenders who turned up to acknowledge his superiority. They decided to give their decision three weeks later. They met in a meadow on the Scots side of the river, where they acceded to Edward's claim.

While prelates and barons accepted Edward's claim, the community rejected it. Edward, in turn, disregarded their rejection. As the pretenders accepted Edward's claim there was less chance of opposition to his title of Lord Superior. The chief claimants were: John de Balliol; Robert de Brus; John Comyn of Badenoch; Florence, Count of Holland; John de Hastings; Lord Abergaveny; Nicholas de Soulis; Patrick de Dunbar, Earl of March; William de Ros; Edward de Pinkeny and William de Vesci. Most of them held lands in England as well as in Scotland, where they were distrusted as aliens and Normans.

1292

At Edward I's request, Balliol and Bruce each chose 42 arbiters and Edward added 24. The decision was not accepted by the Scottish nation, or even the other competitors, so Edward broke the Great Seal of Scotland and substituted a new one. He got the Scottish royal forts under his military forces and added to the number of guardians, ordering them to exact an oath of allegiance from the people of their districts within 15 days. About this time, Edward carried off the records of the kingdom 'though it does not seem that any of them were wilfully destroyed'. Edward then told the Scots that by the law of England the progeny of the elder must be exhausted first and Balliol was chosen in *November* to do 'homage as justly due to Edward as Lord Superior of Scotland'. Balliol accepted the kingdom as Edward's vassal. Edward knew he would and that is why he nominated him. However, the Scots would have no servant of Edward to rule over them.

1296

Because John de Balliol was weak and humiliated Scots pride by his subservience to Edward, he was nicknamed Toom Tabard, meaning 'empty jacket'. Even the weak Balliol rejected Edward's demand of homage. He cited the Treaty of Brigham but was later forced to renounce it and slavishly went to Westminster at Edward's command where he had to stand at the bar like a commoner.

Edward marched north with 30 000 infantry and 5000 cavalry. He defeated the Scots at Dunbar and took its castle. He marched on Edinburgh and took whatever he thought was of worth from its castle. He took the Black Rood or Holy Cross from Holyrood, and sent it to Durham. When he arrived at Scone he took the Coronation Stone, or 'lia-fàil', the 'Stone of Destiny', held in special veneration by the Scots — and sent it to Westminster where it still sits beneath the throne.

1297

A new leader of Scotland arose in the personage of William Wallace. He became a fugitive after slaying an English officer in Dundee. Scottish fighters flocked to his cause and they harassed the English posts in Scotland. They were besieging the castle of Dundee when Wallace received intelligence that the English were heading for Stirling. Wallace went there with his army to meet them.

On *11 September* the English poured over the narrow bridge. They marched over it about noon when Wallace's men seized it at the head. Those English who were over were outnumbered.

1298

Scotland was ravaged by famine and the Scots crossed the border for food and vengeance. Edward I, who had been in Flanders, returned to invade Scotland with 87500 men. Wallace could only muster about one third of that amount. When Edward reached Kirkliston he considered retreat on discovering that the Lothians had become a desert. However, two Scottish knights sent a messenger to him, betraying Wallace's whereabouts. The following day, Edward's army rode to Falkirk where they attacked the Scots. The Scottish knights also betrayed Wallace, turning and riding from the field at a vital moment. Like most of the Scottish nobles they would rather have fought for the English where they believed chivalry was better served.

The Scots army suffered severe slaughter. The retreating body of Wallace's men was too small to hold Stirling and had to pass it by. There was little gain in Edward's victory; he dragged his half-starved army back to Carlisle.

1300

It was the Scottish Church that kept patriotism alive. They were hostile to Edward I for good reason. He ordered that every ecclesiastical office worth 40 merks a year should be given to Englishmen only. The Scots clergy pleaded the case of their country in Rome. Boniface VIII – the Pope during this period who Dante assigned to the lowest parts of hell – sided with Scotland. He sent Edward a bull, clearly and emphatically showing the injustice of his claims.

1305

Wallace was again betrayed by a traitor called Menteith, the governor of Dumbarton. His treachery led to Wallace's capture. Edward was not ungrateful: he paid Menteith 40 merks. Ironically, it was Wallace who was condemned for treason. On *23 August* he was hanged, cut down before he was dead, had his bowels cut out then castrated. His head was cut off and set on London Bridge. His body was quartered and pieces were sent to Berwick, Stirling and Perth to hang to public view.

Edward sought to strike terror into every resisting Scot. He failed. Instead, he deepened their resolve. Edward only created a real emnity towards England that had not previously existed and made union impossible.

1304

A grandson of Robert de Brus, the claimant of the throne against Balliol, arose as another leader. He too was called Robert, best known as Robert the Bruce. He had been trained in Edward's court and, though he received much favour from the English King, was distrusted by him.

Bruce and Lamberton, the Bishop of St Andrews, formed a league at Cambuskenneth, swearing to aid and abet each other against Edward. Edward was informed by John Comyn of Badenoch of this league. Comyn was nearer to the Scottish throne than Bruce, being the son of Balliol's sister, and perhaps feared Bruce's intentions. Bruce was warned by his friend, the Earl of Gloucester, of Edward's intelligence so he fled to Scotland.

1306

When Bobert the Bruce returned to Scotland he met with Comyn in the Church of the Minorite Friars in Dumfries; the month was *February*. There angry words arose between them and Bruce struck Comyn with a sword. He went outside and informed some of his nobles of what had taken place, unsure if Comyn was dead. Sir Roger Kirkpatrick went into the church and ran his sword through the figure lying on the ground to make sure. From that moment Bruce and his men became fugitives, as murder in a church then was considered a greater outrage than murdering 100 men elsewhere.

Bruce was hurriedly crowned at Scone on *27 March*. Although a MacDuff traditionally placed the crown on the head of a Scottish monarch, the MacDuff present kept back. His sister bravely took his place although she was married to a Comyn, the Earl of Buchan, a staunch retainer of Edward. Edward later punished her act by having her hung from a cage on the walls of Berwick.

Edward, residing at Winchester, sent the Earl of Pembroke into Scotland with armed forces. Proclamation was made in the Scottish towns and villages that all armed Scots were to be pursued and hanged or beheaded on capture, and all involved in Comyn's death were to be hung and drawn. Those who would not join in pursuit would be imprisoned and suffer forfeiture.

Pembroke surprised Bruce's army at Methven and, after capturing his castle at Kildrummy, executed his brother Nigel, several relatives and some nobles. Bruce's Queen and daughter were sent to England where they were imprisoned.

1307

Edward I devoted the rest of his days in subduing the Scots. He extracted from his officers a vow that if he died in the enterprise his bones should go with the army and that it should not return until his purpose was fulfilled. But he died at Burgh-on-Sands on the Solway, on *7 July* within sight of Scotland. His son, Edward II, after advancing into Scotland, abandoned the expedition. He returned to England and saw to it that his father's bones were buried at Westminster, next to his wife, Eleanor.

Bruce retook his own castle of Turnberry but he did not hold it for long because of superior force. However, soon afterwards, he defeated Pembroke at Loudon Hill.

1308

The following year showed a favourable turn of events. Comyn of Buchan's men, backed by English soldiers, made a stance at Inverurie. Though Bruce was on his sick bed he rose to go into battle. Its excitement proved better than medicine and Bruce's men won a great victory. The enemy scattered and the pursuit was called 'the Harrying of Buchan'.

Fortresses were rapidly falling to him, often taken by a rising in the district. Though the bishops were generally for him, albeit that most had sworn fealty to Edward, Bruce was still under the Pope's excommunication for killing Comyn.

1314

Within six years the English had lost all their strongholds in Scotland, except for Stirling. The English knew they must hold Stirling or lose all. Mowbray, the governor, was determined to surrender if not relieved by *24 June*.

Bruce realised that, because of the lie of the land and position of the castle, Edward could only approach from the south-east; so he took up the position facing that direction. He placed various groups of his men in advantageous positions. In the level ground – where, he anticipated, the English would veer to evade head-on assault – the Scots dug numerous pits that they covered with turf and brushwood.

On *23 June*, the eve of the battle, Henry de Bohun rode out from the English ranks and challenged Bruce to single combat. Bruce, who was not in full armour but was nevertheless distinguished by a gold circlet around his head, accepted. As de Bohun charged, Bruce, swerving aside from the thrust of his lance, swung round and cleft de Bohun's head with his axe. The handle broke with the force of the blow.

Though his attendants quite rightly blamed him for the rash acceptance, and he offered no excuse, he probably knew that the psychological effect of this opening stroke was worth all the risk.

The following day, *25 June*, as the Scots knelt in prayer before the battle, Edward cried, 'See! They cry for mercy.' One of his knights, who knew them better, is reputed to have replied, 'Yes, but not of you.'

At daybreak, the English archers began the attack. Before they could do any damage, the Scots cavalry charged and scattered them. Then the English advanced into Scottish spears that made their horses unmanageable. As the English pressed forward, there was great confusion in their ranks. When Bruce's line advanced so did a group of camp followers on the crest of a nearby hill. The English mistook them for a fresh army of Scots and began retreating. This inspired the Scots who charged on more resolved; then the English broke into a helpless and hopeless rout. Many of them ran and rode into the pitted fields where they expired.

There were more English dead on the battlefield than there were Scots who entered it. 'A rout so total and unexpected never befel an English army.' All command was lost and no rally was attempted though a force remained large enough to make two armies of equal size to Bruce's.

1319

After being held by the English for 20 years, Berwick was recaptured with more ease than the Scots expected. 'The Siege of Berwick' was raised by the Scots after making a raid into Yorkshire where they defeated the English. The defeated army had been raised by the Archbishop of York and had so many ecclesiastics in its ranks that the battle was called 'the Chapter of Mitton'. The area was so wasted that more than 60 villages and towns were exempted from paying tax. A truce was then made between the Scots and the English and was to last for two years.

1320

Edward made further raids into Scotland and, because the Pope did not recognise Bruce as Scotland's legitimate King nor Scotland's right to independence, the Scots officially drew up a Declaration of Independence, written at Arbroath Abbey and most likely composed by the Abbot, Bernard de Linton, who was also the Chancellor of Scotland. The 'Declaration of Arbroath' was an address to the Pope 'in the most polished and eloquent Latin' urging him not to believe the English and to try to see things from the Scottish viewpoint and, stating that if he did not do so, the carnage inflicted by the Scots on the English and the English on the Scots would continue and that the result, 'we believe, would surely be made by the Most High to your charge'.

The Declaration was written on *6 April* and was endorsed, signed and sealed by 38 Scots lords. A soldier named Randolph took it to Rome where he proved to be an able ambassador. He succeeded in his mission.

1329

The King of the Scots died in his castle at Cardoss on the Clyde after languishing with leprosy on *7 June*. The whole nation of Scotland 'mourned and wept for all knew that a prince and a great man had fallen that day'. His heart was taken out of his body and placed in a casket that the Douglas took with him to the crusades, to be eventually interred in Melrose Abbey. The King's body was then mummified with lead before it was buried in the choir of Dunfermline Abbey.

David II, son of Bruce's second wife, a boy of five years, was crowned at Scone and anointed by the Bishop of St Andrews. This was the first anointing of a Scots King by a Roman Catholic cleric, having been done in previous times by those of the Celtic Church and so had to be sanctified by a special papal bull. The regency was held successfully until 1338 by Randolph, Mar, Murray of Bothwell and Robert the High Steward.

1332

Edward Baliol landed in Fife with a number of discontented barons and defeated the then Regent Mar with a much larger force at Dupplin in Strathearn. Baliol was subsequently crowned at Scone by his followers as a vassal of England. David Bruce, by now a boy of nine years, was sent to the court of Paris for safety by his nobles. Soon after, Baliol was compelled to flee across the border.

1333

Edward III, resolved to invade Scotland, besieged Berwick with such force that the garrison promised to surrender if they were not reinforced by at least 200 men before a certain day. The Scots army returned from a raid into Northumberland to find the English strongly posted and covering Berwick on Halidon Hill. The Scots had to cross a marsh at the foot of the hill where great numbers were cut down by English arrows. The thin numbers that charged up the hill met a crushing defeat, with little loss to the English.

Berwick was forced to surrender and was lost to Scotland more or less for good, except for a few brief periods, though it was not made a part of England. It was provided with a staff of officials for Scotland's government, over which Edward still hoped to extend his lordship. Consequently, Baliol's power was restored and, as a pledge for payment of Edward's aid, his party submitted the south-east counties as far as the Forth, without the sanctions of the Estates of Scotland.

1346

The French encouraged their Scottish allies to invade England. They did in *October* but once again the day was won by English archers. The Scots were utterly defeated and David, six barons, two prelates and the 'Black Rood' were captured. Afterwards, a cross was erected on the battlefield, giving it the name 'Neville's Cross'. Neville, aided by Percy, fought at the battle. They were two great north English noblemen.

1357

David II was not released until this year and only on a ransom of 100000 merks and more than 20 nobles as hostages. David, who had little love for Scotland and indeed hardly saw himself as a Scot, probably found his captivity more pleasant than his throne. He returned to England often and was willing that Edward or Lionel, the English King's son, should succeed him as the King of Scotland. The Scots Estates at once indignantly rejected the proposal.

1371

David II died in Edinburgh Castle on *2 February*. Since he had been a weak King, (almost unbelievably), the son of Robert the Bruce, his death was no great blow to the nation. He was succeeded by Robert II, the son of Bruce's daughter Marjory, who was now 45 years old, though he had for a long time exercised power as King. He was the first of the Stewart line.

1383

A truce that included Scotland was made between France and England but, before news of it reached the Scottish court, the Earls of Northumberland and Nottingham (Percy and Neville) made a raid as far as Edinburgh. Though King Robert accepted the truce, 'the Estates demanded revenge on the two earls despite the King's feelings.'

1388

The Scots replied to an English raid of three years previous in kind. This time, the Scots were the more powerful force. Douglas, with 300 picked lances and 2000 infantrymen advanced as far as Durham to return laden with booty. In Newcastle Douglas took the greatest prize – or loss – to a knight: the pennon of Northumberland's Sir Henry Percy. (Sir Henry was nicknamed 'Hotspur' by the Scots.) Douglas boasted he would place it on his tower at Dalkeith. Hotspur vowed it would never leave Northumberland and Douglas challenged him to take it from his tent that night if he dared.

The English barons restrained him from so foolhardy an attempt. They suspected it to be a trap leading them into an ambush by a supporting army of Scots, for they had no intelligence as to the size of the Douglas' force.

However, on *19 August* both sides met and fought in the moonlight. This was known as 'the Battle of Otterburn' or 'the Chevy Chase', in an English ballad of that name. Hotspur was taken prisoner and Douglas died; he was trodden on by his own men when he fell. According to the ballad, the English won a great victory though, in fact, it belonged to the Scots.

1390

Robert II died in his castle of Dundonald, near Irvine, in Ayrshire. He was a peaceable man but often found himself surrounded by unruly nobles in troubled times. He was succeeded by his son, John, but since this name was considered too odious for a Scottish King, he was given the popular one of Robert, although it was already borne by his younger brother.

1398

The Estates of Scotland set about bringing tyrannical nobles to heel by making the King responsible for their behaviour. This was to give the ordinary people the right to denounce the oppression they could not prevent. The same Estates, during the same year, introduced a new title into Scotland: the King's brother was made the Duke of Albany and his eldest son the Duke of Rothesay. They were given accompanying powers to 'restrain distasteful misdoers, cursed men and heretics, and those thrust forth from the church'. This implies that the doctrines of Wycliffe and the Lollards had affected Scotland at that time.

1400

Henry IV invaded Scotland with a large force. They advanced as far as Leith. They could not have met any kind of violent resistance, that was normal for those times, because Henry decided to return with his troops to England without inflicting any damage.

1402

The young Duke of Rothesay was a wild and reckless profligate. A great hatred grew between him and his uncle, Albany. Each wanted to have the King in his hands so he could wield the power of the state. Since his conduct required restraint, although it abetted the designs of his uncle, he was seized and imprisoned in Falkland Palace. Though it was never clear what happened to him it was certain that he stood in Albany's way and that his death happened while he was in his uncle's power. His body was found to be wasted to a skeleton. The general view that he was starved to death is the most likely. There is an old story that may actually go back to that time claiming he was so starved that he ate his own hands.

That same year after Douglas and an army of 10 000 men had sacked Durham and were returning with great plunder, Hotspur and March met them near Wooler. Though the Scots took a strong position on Homildon Hill, the Percy was all for an immediate attack. March, who knew their strengths and weaknesses, was against it. Instead, he made use of his archers who fired on the dense mass of soldiers, causing great havoc. Though two Scots nobles with about 100 retainers made a brave charge, they were all cut down. The Scots were defeated and Douglas captured. However, the English claimed that had the rest fought as bravely as those who charged, the battle's result would have been very different.

1405

As Albany had got rid of the King's son there was concern that he had designs against the other James, a youth of 14. Prudence demanded that the Prince James be put out of the Duke's reach. For Albany, not the ineffectual King, was the real ruler of the nation. So the young Prince was sent to the court of France for protection and tutelage.

He sailed out of the Forth in *March*, with a suitable retinue, only to be captured by an English warship off Flamborough Head. As this was a time of truce, the English must have been given intelligence through agents of Albany.

27

1411

Donald, Lord of the Isles, declared war on the Lowlands because his claims to the Earldom of Ross were rejected by Mar and the government. Like his ancestors, some of whom had sided with the English kings against their own, he hardly regarded the Stewarts as his monarchs. With a force of 10000 men he attacked the Lowlanders of Harlaw. The fight was so severe, and the victory so important, that certain privileges were granted to the heirs of the fallen.

1424

James J was released on giving hostages for the payment of £40000 for his keep in captivity. One-fourth was remitted as a dowry for his Queen, the daughter of Henry, his jailer. He returned to rule Scotland.

1427

Donald of the Isles and 50 other chiefs were seized and several of them executed. Donald was spared because he submitted to the government though he soon rebelled again, destroying Inverness. In 1431 he plundered Lochaber.

1437

James I was brutally murdered on *20 February* in the residence of the Dominican monastery in Perth. Though he tried to hide from his assailants in a secret passage under a fireplace, he was discovered and stabbed to death by Sir John Hall, Hall's brother, and Sir Robert Graham. These Lowland nobles who broke into the residence were backed by 300 Highlanders. The King might have escaped had he not had the garden entrance to the passage bricked up a few days before, in order to stop tennis balls falling in.

The murderers paid for their crime severely, 'that were to any mankind too sorrowful and piteous a sight, and too abominable to see'. Graham was paraded through the town of Stirling on the back of a cart with his hand nailed to a post by the sword he used to kill the King. His hand was cut off by the same sword just prior to his being stripped naked for men to tear at almost every inch of his flesh from his hair to his feet.

Before they finally executed him, they disembowelled his living son in front of his eyes.

1440

The Douglases had been a powerful family who were even feared by the monarchs; they themselves had a claim to the throne. Sir William Crichton, who feared and mistrusted them, invited Lord James Douglas to Edinburgh Castle. Proud and defiant, he not only accepted the invitation but he took his brother along. While they dined, a bull's head on a silver salver was placed on the table, which served as a signal for armed men to seize them. They were both taken into the court-yard where they were beheaded.

1451

Glasgow University was established in 1451 by a Bull of Pope Nicholas V as a *'stadium generale* in theology, canon, civil law, and any other lawful faculty'. The Bull was given on request of King James II and the King in turn granted his 'dear daughter', the university, an exemption from taxes in 1453. The founder and first chancellor was William Turnbull, Bishop of Glasgow.

1452

William, the son and heir of Earl James, rose to promi-nence and made friends with his house's enemies, Crichton included. He became the lieutenant of the realm. The King, desiring a personal conference, invited him to Stirling Castle under a 'safe conduct'.

After a meal the King told him to break with the bands of other unruly nobles who were his allies. On refusing, the King drew a dagger and stabbed him twice, before Sir Patrick Grey felled him with a pole-axe. The bleeding body was then thrown from the chamber window into the courtyard far below.

1457

An act was passed in *March* 'that the Fute-ball and Golf be utterly cryit doune, and not usit'.

1460

Though there was a truce with England, the Scots thought it an opportune time to invade as England was enduring the Wars of the Roses. It was a good opportunity for them to recover Roxburgh and Berwick; they considered them their own anyway.

At the siege of Roxburgh, a cannon exploded and part of it hit the King. James II died instantly; it was *2 August*. James III was crowned, though he was not yet eight years old. His government was directed by Bishop Kennedy until the bishop's death five years later.

1469

The royal marriage took place under peculiar circumstances: the yearly sum for the Western Isles of 100 merks, ceded by Norway after the Battle of Largs, had never been paid. The 200 years' arrears made an enormous sum and Christian I of Norway, Sweden and Denmark wanted it to be paid. The Scots could not afford it so they settled the matter amicably: James III needed a wife, and Christian wanted a husband for his daughter. Thus, they were to be married and as a dowry Christian would cancel his claim to the Hebrides plus give £5000. He never got round to paying the debt so Orkney and Shetland were placed under Scots keeping as a pledge for payment. They are still waiting!

1471

The see of St Andrews was made an archbishopric but the first two Archbishops angered the Estates by taking too many of the nation's affairs to the Pope. The Estates then ordained, under the pain of treason, that none should apply to Rome for appointments to any abbacies or benefices that were not by their original constitution in the gift of Rome, and all who had taken pleas there were to bring them home for settlement by courts of law.

In *May* another act decreed that 'the Fute-ball and Golfe be abusit in tyme cuming!'.

1482

The King's favourite, Cochrane, who was either a stonemason or an architect, became so familiar with the King that the nobles were outraged. He is said even to have set the King against his own brothers. Cochrane was taken with a few other of the King's favourites by the Earl of Angus and other nobles, and hanged over Lauder Bridge in front of the King's eyes.

1488

The Estates charged James III with surrounding himself with evil advisers who were assisting him in 'the inbringing of Englishmen' into the realm. A confederacy was formed and an army rose to meet his forces at Sauchieburn, near Bannockburn in *June*. The King fled from the battle but his horse threw him. A woman finding him lay him on her bed and called for a priest. A man soon presented himself as one and, pretending to hear his confession, leaned over him and stabbed him to death. Soon after, James IV was crowned as King.

1491

It was ordained in *May* that in 'no place of the realm there be usit Fute-ball, Golfe or other unprofitabill sportis.' Despite these parliamentary bans James IV, James V and Mary Queen of Scots – who was charged with playing a few days after her husband's murder – were all keen golfers. James VI played on Blackheath Common.

1500

Hector Boece, the Dundee-born scholar and historian, was summoned from Paris by Bishop William Elphinstone to be the first principal of Aberdeen University. The university dates from 1494-95 when, at the instigation of Elphinstone, Pope Alexander VI (the notorious Borgia Pope) granted a Bull.

1502

King Ferdinand of Spain at first did not know whether to give his daughter to the son of the King of England or to Scotland's King. He eventually opted for England. The English King, Henry VII, in turn gave his daughter, Margaret, to James and both were married at Lamberton Church that midsummer. ' . . . the marriage of Margaret 101 years afterwards made of two opposing and warring nations one great Protestant people.'

1507

Printing was introduced into Scotland by Walter Chapman, a servant in the royal household. As the King was 'the ready patron of every new invention or curious art' he granted Chapman a patent, paid for his books, and encouraged him in every way. The following year, with his partner Myllar, Chapman published the first collection of Dunbar's poems.

1513

James IV led his country to disaster because of ridiculous notions of chivalry. The French Queen sent him 15000 crowns with a letter saying she was a doleful lady with an enemy at her door and, as her 'chosen knight', charged him to march for her 'three feet into English ground'.

So James crossed with the force of the realm into England, taking Wark then Norham Castle. The English met them on the great crest of Flodden and, though it was an excellent defensive position for the Scots, the four English divisions broke the five Scottish.

The battle began at four o'clock in the afternoon of Friday *9 September*. It was a disaster for Scotland. A king, two prelates, 25 lords and 10000 men fell in the fight. There were few families, indeed, in Scotland who had not lost a member at 'Dark Flodden'. If the Scots showed little skill or prudence in the battle they did at least fight bravely. Though the result was a calamity for Scotland it was not a disgrace.

The crown fell to James V, an infant of 16 months, when the heads of the great families and rulers of the towns had fallen in battle. Everything was in new hands – untried and untrained.

1522

John Knox enrolled at Glasgow University on St Crispin's day, *25 October*. He was attracted to the university by the fame of the great Scots scholar, John Major, who was himself born near Knox's birthplace at Haddington, and was probably educated at the same burgh school as Knox. Major, however, left Glasgow the following June because he was transferred to St Andrews. Unless Knox followed him there (and there is no proof that he did, for his name does not appear on either of those universities' records as a graduate), he can only have been his pupil for one session.

The death of the poet Gawin Douglas occurred. He was the third son of Archibald, the Earl of Angus, and like many educated Scots of that time he had travelled and studied in Europe. He was, in many ways, an inferior poet to his contemporaries and elders, Robert Henrysoun and William Dunbar.

1528

Patrick Hamilton, the preacher of the Reformed Doctrine, returned to Scotland after living as an exile in Germany. He fled there after Cardinal Beaton had scrutinised his teachings and pronounced him 'worthy of death'. On his return, Beaton deprived him of all Church offices and handed him over to the civil power. Hamilton was burned at the stake in front of the old college of St Andrews.

1542

Four years after James V had married Mary of Lorraine, Norfolk's forces were sent into Scotland to punish him for a slight given to the English King. Home met the forces at Jedburgh and defeated them. Another English army of 30 000 was sent. James led an army southwards, under the command of Oliver Sinclair. There was indignance and confusion at Sinclair's commission and, observing it, the English charged the Scottish camp. James was ill with vexation after the defeat and was also ill with low fever. He was removed to Falkland Palace where he grew worse. On hearing of the birth of his daughter he said of the Scottish crown: 'It cam wi' a lass and it will gang wi' a lass'. He died on *14 December* in his 31st year.

As Mary, the King's daughter, was only a week old the country came under the regency of the Earl of Arran, a descendant of James II and next in line to the throne. Beaton produced a will entrusting the royal child to him; it was rejected as a forgery and the charge of Mary was given to her mother.

1546

George Wishart, a native of the Mearns, was apprehended by Earl Bothwell at Ormiston for preaching the Reformed Doctrines in Dundee, Ayr and the Lothians. He had been accused of heresy two years before while teaching at the School for Classic Tongues in Montrose and had fled to England where he taught at Cambridge. He was sent to St Andrews where he was burned at the stake by an irregular trial and without the sanction of the civil power. The execution took place in front of Cardinal Beaton's castle where he looked on exultingly.

On the morning of *29 May* Norman Leslie, the son of Lord Rothes, James Melville, Kirkcaldy of Grange and about five others, entered Beaton's castle and slew him. When a crowd of Beaton's diocesans marched outside the castle demanding to see their cardinal, the assassins held his gashed body over the ramparts to show how they had taken revenge for his persecution of the Protestants. The crowd quickly dispersed.

1547

Henry VIII died that year but his policy was carried on by the Duke of Somerset, Protector of England and uncle of young King Edward. He invaded Scotland with 15 000 men, backed by a fleet. He devastated the Scots on *10 September*, putting them to flight at the Battle of Pinkie. More fell in the flight than in the actual battle. Before he returned to London he destroyed the church of Holyrood Abbey and did other damage around Edinburgh.

1548

The six-year-old Mary Queen of Scots was not considered safe from the English in any Scottish castle. Knowing that as long as she was in the country the English would invade it, the Scots resolved to send her to France. The French fleet sailed quite openly around the north and west coasts of Scotland, stopping at Dumbarton to pick Mary up. Having done so they landed her safely at Brest on *30 August*.

1554

On *12 April* Mary of Guise, the Queen's mother, was made regent instead of the Earl of Arran. However, she conferred on the earl the French dukedom of Chatelherault. Though she had been 16 years in Scotland she did not understand the feelings of the people: she placed several Frenchmen in important positions, although the Scots had always been intolerant of foreigners holding offices of trust in the country.

1555

Sir David Lyndsay, the poet and tutor of the young James V, and the Lyon King of Arms, died during this year.

1558

Mary Queen of Scots' first marriage was to the French Dauphin on *24 April*. Though six Scots commissioners in France did their utmost to preserve the separate nationality of their country, Mary 'signed away Scotland, its rights and its revenues as if dealing with her private property'. Her husband took the title of King of Scots and demanded the regalia. On their journey home, three of the commissioners died and many in Scotland believed the French court 'took means to prevent these men carrying home the knowledge they acquired'.

1559

Henry II of France died after he was wounded at a tournament. Mary's husband succeeded as Francis II and, as Mary was their Queen now, the French court acted as if Scotland was one of its provinces.

After being in charge of the English Church at Geneva, where he formed an intimacy with Calvin, John Knox returned to Scotland on *2 May*. Soon after his return, the reformers became the controlling power in Scotland.

1560

Mary not only lost her mother but, on *15 December*, her husband as well. At that time the Scots wanted her to return home, hoping that if she did the country would escape from the influence of France and the Guises. Both the Protestants and the Catholics hoped to win her to their side.

1561

Mary arrived at Leith on *19 August* but preparations for her reception had not been completed. She had to wait for horses to arrive since there were not any carriages. When they finally did arrive, she had to go to Holyrood on horseback.

1565

Though Mary would have preferred to marry Don Carlos, heir to the Spanish throne, her cousin Henry Stewart, Lord Darnley, came to her from England where he was first prince of the blood. Within three months she announced her marriage to him to an assembly at Stirling. He was made Earl of Ross and Duke of Albany and, on *29 July*, he married her. Without calling a parliament, Mary proclaimed Darnley King of the Scots.

1566

Mary's love for her husband soon cooled. He became jealous of one of her favourites, David Rizzio, who had entered her service as a musician but was soon after appointed as her private foreign secretary in *1564*. Darnley's jealous suspicions were stirred by the fact that Rizzio was often in the Queen's chamber and had his own bedchamber directly beneath hers with a private staircase leading up to it.

On *9 March*, Darnley led Lord Ruthven and some others into a chamber where Mary, with some other attendants, was entertaining Lady Argyll and Rizzio. Rizzio was dragged from the Queen, to whom he had been clinging in terror, screaming and kicking. He was stabbed to death at the door of the Queen's chamber. Mary was pregnant at the time and, on *19 June*, gave birth to her son James VI.

1567

Mary now had another lover, James Hepburn, the fourth Earl of Bothwell. She plotted with him to murder Darnley. The King, who was ill at that time, was convalescing in Edinburgh in an old house formerly the residence of the provost of the religious house of St Mary in the Fields and called Kirk o' the Fields. The bedroom directly under the King's was packed with barrels of gunpowder by Bothwell's accomplices. On the night of *9 February*, a fuse was lit and the building was blown apart. Darnley's body was thrown a great height into the air and it is likely he died from the fall as there were not any burn marks on his body. The mattress underneath him most likely protected him from the blast.

Bothwell was created Duke of Orkney and Shetland on *12 May*; three days later, he married Mary.

On *24 July* Mary signed three documents; renouncing the crown in favour of her son, appointing Moray as regent and naming several lords as a collective regency until Moray returned to Scotland. James VI was crowned on *29 July* in the High Church at Stirling.

1568

It was generally believed that Mary was guilty of the murder of Darnley and the people of Scotland wanted her to stand trial. The Scots council sympathised with the people and five of the conspirators in Darnley's murder were hanged.

Mary was imprisoned in Lochleven Castle but, with the help of accomplices, escaped. The next morning they had got as far as Hamilton Palace, accompanied by growing numbers that soon increased to 6000.

Moray, who had been called upon by Mary's party to resign his regency, gathered 4500 troops at Glasgow. About two miles south of the city, at Langside, they met Mary's force on *13 May* and defeated them. Mary fled to England, entering it on the *16 May*.

Mary was soon involved in intrigues and, though a prisoner, enjoyed a relative amount of freedom and still lived like a queen. Elizabeth merely kept her confined until she had been cleared of her husband's death and, if exonerated, Elizabeth would replace her with full powers and endeavour to put her on the throne, albeit jointly with her son.

The Scottish party represented by Moray produced damaging letters – known as 'the Casket Letters' – supposedly written in Mary's own hand and showing her involvement in her husband's murder.

1569

Mary took revenge against Moray through her allies the Hamiltons. As Moray rode through Linlithgow, on *23 January*, James Hamilton of Bothwellhaugh waited to commit a cowardly murder from the house of Archbishop Hamilton. Though Moray had been warned that there would be an attempt on his life, he openly rode through the streets where he must have known he would be thronged by a crowd, as indeed he was. The cheering crowd gathered round him, slowing his horse and giving the assassin time to take aim and fire. The bullet passed through the regent's body and killed a horse. The murderer escaped through a back garden where a horse was waiting for him. Lennox, who came from England and spent most of his time there was made the next regent.

1571

The death of Moray led to a succession of regents, reckoned to be a period that was 'about the most deplorable in Scottish history'. The Scots and the Kerrs made a raid into England and Elizabeth replied by invading the south and Clydeside. Maitland and Kirkcaldy of Grange took Edinburgh Castle for Mary, but Dumbarton was taken for her son by Thomas Crawford of Jordanhill with the assistance of 100 volunteers from Glasgow. They took it on *2 April* without losing a man. They took much spoil and captured Archbishop Hamilton who was executed at Stirling five days later. The parliament met at Stirling in *August* and soon afterward the Earl of Huntly, with 380 horsemen and 380 musketeers, seized the town. However, his men soon broke up to plunder and the garrison were roused and defeated them. Regent Lennox was shot in the uproar and Mar became the next regent.

1572

Though no one great battle was fought there were many warring factions in the nation. The bulk of the Lowlands was for the King though the Hamiltons, Maxwells and Kerrs split the west and south for Mary while Huntly tyrannised the north for her. Grange held on to Edinburgh, menacing the city from the castle with guns; he had others planted on the tower of St Giles. The King's party held Leith with a battery on Calton Hill. Intimidated citizens fled from the capital and John Knox moved to St Andrews.

A truce between the two parties was made in *August* for two months, although it lasted for the rest of the year. John Knox returned during the truce but died on *24 November*.

The news of the St Bartholomew's Day Massacre in Paris on *25 August* – when Pope Gregory XIII ordered the slaughter of 10000 Huguenots and had a coin struck celebrating the event – filled the nation with so much horror that the people became more Presbyterian. Grange put up an obstinate stand but actually surrendered and was hanged at the Mercat Cross on *3 August*. Mar died in October and was succeeded by Morton.

1581

Morton accrued a lot of wealth through his office and, in doing so, a lot of enemies likewise. Though an able ruler, he was generally disliked and when he was accused of being involved in the plot to murder

Darnley, could not get a noble to take his part. He was beheaded on *2 June* by the Maiden, an early version of the guillotine that, ironically, he had personally introduced into Scotland.

No-one succeeded Morton and the government was conducted, nominally, by James. When he was hunting at the Earl of Gowrie's castle near Perth on *22 August* he found himself surrounded by several nobles and 1000 armed men; this is known to history as the 'Raid of Ruthven'. The King was free to go where he wanted but was always escorted, for ten months, by well-armed followers. The 'Raid of Ruthven' was planned to deliver him from the power and influence of Lennox and Arran. However, Arran was imprisoned and Lennox fled to France.

1582

George Buchanan, the greatest scholar of his day, besides being a patriot and poet, died on *28 September*. He was James' teacher and helped to make him a scholar far beyond the princes of his time. As a child of eight, James could translate a chapter of the Latin Bible into French and English.

1583

Edinburgh University, the 'youngest of the old Scottish universities', was founded a year after James VI's charter of 1582 by the local town council. The first buildings of the 'tounis colledge' were erected on the grounds of the ill-famed Kirk o' the Field.

1584

While the King was at St Andrews, Huntly, Marischall and Argyll, backed by superior forces, delivered the King from a control that had been highly approved of by the Estates and the General Assembly. Most of the 'Ruthven' lairds escaped to England but Gowrie was executed and Arran rose to his former power.

1586

Though Mary Queen of Scots was allowed a large household and had £30000 a year as Dowager of France 'she was ever intriguing with wonderful ability and unwearied labour'. But the final plot that proved fatal to her was the 'Babington Conspiracy' headed by Antony Babington, a rich young Derbyshire Catholic. Its object was twofold: to murder Elizabeth and rescue Mary. The plot was discovered and Babington was executed on *20 September*. Thirteen other conspirators met a similar fate.

Mary's complicity was evident in letters written in her hand. She denied they were hers and Elizabeth seemed reluctant to prosecute her but her nobles demanded that Mary be brought to trial. They were heeded and Mary was put on trial on *14 October* at Fotheringay for conspiracy against Elizabeth's life.

The trial was postponed at the end of the second day until *25 October* when commissioners met in the Star Chamber at Westminster and passed the death sentence on her. A few days later the English parliament confirmed the sentence, petitioning Elizabeth to sanction its execution, urging that, 'if she had no regard for her own life, she had duties to the throne, the freedom of England, and the safety of its religion.' She answered evasively, even though the English council confirmed and published the sentence in *December*.

1587

Elizabeth I finally and reluctantly gave the warrant on *1 February*. Soon after she tried to recall it but it was too late and Mary was beheaded on *8 February* in the castle hall of Fotheringay. She was buried, with honours, beside Catherine of Aragon.

When James VI became of age on *19 June* he invited his nobles to a great banquet with the intention of securing peace. He attempted this by ordering the greatest foes amongst them to march in pairs from the palace to the Mercat Cross, along the Royal Mile.

1589

Anne, second daughter of the King of Denmark, sailed to Scotland to be James' wife. However, contrary winds drove her ship into Norway, detaining her so that James personally sailed to Norway to bring her back. He met her at Uppsala in Sweden where they were married on *23 November*.

1590

James VI arrived at Leith with his Queen on *1 May*, accompanied by a retinue of Danish lords and ladies. James decided to remain for so long in Scandinavia to avoid a winter crossing.

1592

The Estates passed an act to abolish bishoprics, giving the government of the Church to kirk sessions, presbyteries, and synods, with appeals through these to the General Assembly – the supreme Church court. It was presided over by the King or his commissioner. This was the beginning of the power of the Presbyterian Church in Scotland.

1600

1 January was made the first day of the year. Prior to then it began on *25 March* (the beginning of spring). The English did not make that alteration until 1752.

On *5 August*, according to James, the Master of Ruthven and his brother Lord Gowrie made an attempt on his life at their home in Perth. They were slain for the attempt. The story was not made known at the time and there was an uproar at Perth where the two men were popular. Though many considered the King's story of the 'Gowrie Conspiracy' to be too aimless to be believed, 'the Estates decreed the name and dignity of the Gowrie to be extinguished'. More than likely, the King had them murdered out of fear that they would want revenge for their father's death, ordered by James for his involvement with the 'Raid of Ruthven'.

1603

James was wakened late on the night of *Saturday 26 March* by Sir Robert Carey who told him he was King of England. Carey had travelled from Richmond Palace where his sister, one of Elizabeth's ladies-in-waiting, dropped him a ring from a window as the signal. She took it from Elizabeth's finger just as she died. It happened at 3 am on *Thursday 24 March*, and Carey rode with the tidings to Edinburgh.

James, who left the capital with a great train, was received at Berwick with great honours. He was 'sumptuously entertained' on his southward journey and, during the month it took, appointed about 150 knights before reaching London. Though some of his Scottish nobles followed to London, few received any great office. Many were refused as much as an audience with him.

1605

Many in England thought that James had no right to succeed the throne, and considered his cousin, Arabella Stuart, to be the rightful heir. The Puritans, who corresponded with him, thought the Reformation incomplete, while the Catholics wanted it undone. Feeling cheated, the Catholics planned the famous gunpowder plot on *5 November* with Guy Fawkes at the helm. The day they chose for blowing up parliament was when the King would be there.

1606

The Estates sanctioned plans for the reconstruction of the Episcopy and the bishops were restored to their offices. Though they were later made moderators of the Synods, their livings were mostly now in the hands of laymen who would not surrender them.

1607

As a result of the union of the crowns the Border laws were abolished and the peoples of both England and Scotland could claim citizenship of either country. John Welsh, with 18 others, held an assembly at Aberdeen without the King's consent and all were charged with treason. In Scotland it simply meant disobedience to an order of court resulting in a fine. For their crime they were ordered to be banished from Scotland.

1616-1617

John Napier, who was so brilliant a mathematician that his contemporaries thought him a practitioner of the black arts, died at Merchiston Castle, Edinburgh on *4 April*. This inventor of impractical military gadgetry was best known for inventing the mathematical system of logarithms – an innovation that had a profound effect on science until well into the present century. His book on the subject, *Logarithmorum Canonis Constructio* was not published until two years after his death.

James came back to Scotland in *May 1616* and spent 15 months in royal pageants. In 1617 he attended a meeting of the Estates where deans were restored to their sees. It was also decreed there that all ministers should receive stipends of from 500 to 800 merks.

1618

The Assembly at Perth passed the 'Five Articles' expressing James' views: kneeling at communion in public, private communion to the sick, private baptism when necessary, confirmation by the bishops of eight-year-old children, and the observance of Christmas, Good Friday, Easter, Ascension Day and Whitsun Day. They were offensive to many, although there were no penalties for disobedience.

1622

The colony of Nova Scotia was founded a year after the Earl of Stirling was given a grant of its land. Scots settled in the new colony and whoever took charge of one of its 1000 allotments was to be created a baron.

1624

George Heriot, who had followed James to London as a court jeweller and banker, died and left his wealth to found a hospital in Edinburgh for 'the maintenance of and education of sons of poor deceased or decaying burgesses'. The building was completed in 1642.

1625

James VI died on *27 March*, about 13 years after the death of his eldest son Henry. His second son, born in Dunfermline in 1600, succeeded him as Charles I.

1628

One of Charles I' first acts in Scotland was the revocation of Church lands. The act alarmed the landowners.

1633

A settlement of the dispute the act caused was not effected until this year when most holders of Church property resigned a portion of it to receive a clear title to the remainder. Charles I was crowned in *June* with great pomp and ceremony in Holyrood Abbey. He was crowned King of England at Westminster on *2 February 1626*. He was accompanied by Laud, the Archbishop of Canterbury, who tried to make the Church nearer to Rome than the bishops wished. His ambitions must have pleased Charles who was a hater of Puritanism and a lover of ritual.

1636

Laud prepared some canons and ecclesiastical constitutions that Charles issued on his own authority. He did not consult the council, Estates, or even the bishops about it, though they had been preparing a different set. The aristocracy resented the interference with their lands as well as with the power and rights of the Estates. The Presbyterians resisted episcopal rule and ceremonies, and the nation generally opposed an attempt to force English ways upon them.

1637

The spark that ignited the temper of the nation was a service book prepared by Laud and imposed by the King. Compared to the English liturgy it was 'more Romish, both in its additions and its omissions'. It was enforced 'under pain of outlawry, and its appearance was like an illustrated Roman Catholic breviary or missal'. Its use was intended for Easter but it was wisely delayed on the council's advice. An order was issued that all ministers must use it from *Sunday 21 July* or otherwise be 'put to the horn' and thus treated as rebels against the King and law.

No sooner had the dean opened it at St Giles in Edinburgh, watched by the Archbishop of St Andrews and the Bishop of Edinburgh, when a confused murmur arose. Jenny Geddes, keeper of a cabbage stall at the Tron, called out, 'Oot ye false thief! Wad ye say mass at my lug?' and she threw the stool, on which she had

45

been sitting, at the dean. Others joined in throwing their stools and books. Though the rioters were eventually expelled from the church, they kept roaring and battering at the doors until the service ended.

The hostility against the prayer books grew and numbers of protesters thronged from all parts to Edinburgh. Charles issued a proclamation on *17 October* commanding all to depart from the city who had no business there, and he denounced a popular book written by George Gillespie, entitled: *Dispute Against the English-Popish Ceremonies Obtruded on the Church of Scotland*. In reply, a petition was presented to the King from 'noblemen, barons, ministers, burgesses and commons'. It became famous as the 'Supplication' and its supporters were called 'Supplicants'.

Early in *December* the King issued a proclamation, sternly condemning the Supplicants while stating his abhorrence of popery. The Supplicants retorted with their famous 'Protestation'. Wherever the King's proclamation was read, it was immediately followed by the Protestation. Aberdeen was the only place, outside of Highland territory, where it did not receive full sympathy of the people. Because of these readings and counter-readings, Johnston of Warriston suggested that the National Covenant of 1557, with some additions, be renewed so that the Supplicants could bind themselves 'to defend their religious liberties'.

1638

This was done and multitudes of people of all classes signed the Covenant on *1 March* in Greyfriars Churchyard, Edinburgh. These Supplicants from then on were, and still are, known as the Covenanters. The King eventually sent his relation, the Marquis of Hamilton, to them to hear their demands and issue a proclamation. It is said he met 500 ministers and 20000 people in an area between Leith and Musselburgh. In the proclamation the King neither yielded to nor refused the people's claims. But in his private instructions he wrote to Hamilton, 'Flatter the people with what hopes you please' but '. . . I will rather die than yield to those impertinent demands.' He also stated, 'I do not expect that you should declare the adherents of the Covenant traitors, until you have heard from me that my fleet hath set sail for Scotland.'

An assembly met in Glasgow on *21 September* in Glasgow Cathedral. Hamilton, the commissioner, pronounced it dissolved for excluding the bishops and admitting laymen. The assembly ignored his pronouncement and carried on with business, abolishing the Articles of Perth, the canons and the service book. It excommunicated eight of the prelates and deposed the other six.

1639

The Covenant was not popular in the north where Huntly acted for the King. James Graham, then Earl of Montrose, was sent to Aberdeen first as a leader of a deputation to reason the people into signing it. In *February* he returned as the leader of an army, to subdue them to its cause. Huntly submitted to him and went with him to Edinburgh where Montrose imprisoned him in the castle.

The Covenanters soon had command of the country; Edinburgh Castle and other fortresses fell into their hands and the Estates declined to issue the King's proclamation of war. At the beginning of *May*, Hamilton sailed into the Forth with a fleet of 19 ships carrying five regiments but they were unable to land. The King came to Berwick on *1 June* with an army but David Leslie, in command of 22000 foot soldiers and 500 on horse, occupied Duns Law to bar entrance to Scotland. Charles knew a fight was impossible so he negotiated instead, promising once more a free parliament and assembly. He soon after won Montrose to his cause, though, in his heart, he remained a Covenanter.

1640

David Leslie mustered 22000 men at Dunglass, crossed the Tweed at Coldstream on *20 August* and marched to Newcastle. He entered the by then fortified town by clearing a passage from Newburn, five miles above Newcastle. He paid for the supplies he took locally, though only with money he levied – gift bonds for some indefinite future payment.

1641

Having no force to oppose them Charles I began a treaty at Ripon that was concluded at London in *August*. He also visited Scotland, making Leslie the Earl of Leven, raising Argyll to the rank of Marquis, and sanctioning all that the Estates asked. At the same time he was in a plot with Montrose, had a plan for the seizure of Argyll and several others and stirred the Irish into a rising that went further than he intended: it ended in a massacre of almost all of the English in Dublin.

1642

There was civil war in England with the Royalists versus the Long Parliament, the latter siding with the Covenanters. Charles set up his standard at Nottingham and his forces held Newcastle, thereby managing to halt the supply of coals to London, the centre of opposition. The English parliament made an alliance with the Scots and took their army into pay.

1644

Leslie crossed the Tweed on *19 January*, crossed the Tyne near Newcastle, drove the Royalists back to Durham, returned to Newcastle and left a sufficient force to carry on with the siege. With the main body of his army, he marched to Tadcaster where they joined the parliamentary forces. Their united force marched to York, held by the Royalists, intent on taking it but Prince Rupert gave them battle at Marston Moor, five miles west of the city, on *26 July*. The parliamentary forces were the victors, due mainly to the skills of the generals Leslie and Cromwell.

Though the King's cause seemed lost, Montrose revived its hopes. With 1200 Irish he raised his standard at Atholl, marched on Perth, routed Lord Elcho at Tibbermore on *1 September*, and held the town for three days. He then marched on Aberdeen and defeated the Covenanters on *13 September* to pillage the city.

1645

On *2 February* Montrose surprised Argyll at Inverlochie where he slew 1500 Campbells and scattered the rest, losing only four of his own men. He then marched north-west and was lost sight of until he reappeared at Dundee. General Urry, an experienced soldier, attacked him at Auldearn, near Nairn, and was defeated – as was Baillie who tried a similar attack at Alford. Next, Montrose held the Campsie Fells and then, on *15 August* completely routed Baillie at Kilsyth 'that scarcely an unmounted Covenanter escaped'. He then moved south-west, sweeping all before him.

David Leslie returned to Scotland, entering at Berwick and turning south to meet Montrose. Montrose was in his headquarters at Selkirk while his men were camped at Philiphaugh. Knowing their positions, Leslie attacked on the morning of *13 September*, dividing Montrose's forces. On hearing the fire, Montrose hastened to the battleground where his army had perished without a fight. 'His brilliant career of a year and a few days was over.'

1646

When Oxford fell – where Charles had confined himself after a defeat at Naseby (*14 June 1645*) – and a safe conduct was denied him, he walked into the Scots lines at Newark on *5 May*. When asked to surrender him the Scots retired to Newcastle, holding him until their affairs with parliament were settled.

1647

On *8 January* the Scots received £400000 on agreeing to deliver the King to the commissioners of parliament. They could scarcely retain an English King in England against the will of the parliament that had invited them into the country.

1649

Charles I was tried for high treason and was beheaded on *30 January*. His death was chiefly due to the belief of his opponents that the sparing of his life would result in the loss of their own. On hearing of his execution, the Scots immediately proclaimed his son, Charles II, King on *5 February* on condition that he 'would espouse God's cause'. He accepted their conditions while still urging Montrose to war with them.

1650

Both Huntly and Montrose were executed. Montrose had landed in the north in *March* but failed to raise the Highlands. The few who did fight with him were routed at Invercarron in Ross-shire, leaving him to roam the hills until he was taken, half-starved, by MacLeod of Assynt who was out with a party searching for him. He was taken to Edinburgh and there on *21 May* 'perverse and brave' Montrose was hung, drawn and quartered.

Charles II landed at the mouth of the Spey on *3 July*. Though he had signed the Covenant the Scots felt that they could fight for him better if he were *not* in their midst.

Cromwell marched into Scotland with an army of 16 000 crack troops. Though Leslie's were inferior, they covered Edinburgh with such skill that Cromwell saw an attack on it would be futile, so he withdrew with his starving army to Dunbar. Though Leslie's men surrounded them and Cromwell himself wrote that his men could not get through them 'without a miracle', to his joy and surprise, the Scots moved to a plain on Lammermoors. He got his men to charge in the morning of *3 September* before the Scots had well formed. He later wrote, 'in less than an hour's dispute, their whole army being put into confusion, became a total rout, our men having the chase and execution of them near eight miles'. Three thousand Scots were slain and 10 000 were taken prisoner.

1651

Though Cromwell was now master of all Scotland south of the Forth, the Scots did not yield; they crowned Charles at Scone on *1 January*, Argyll putting the crown on his head. Cromwell tried to induce Leslie to fight but, not succeeding, he withdrew to Perth. The Scots immediately marched into England but received little help from the Royalists there. Cromwell met them at Worcester on *3 September* but Charles fled with a few followers before the battle had even ended, though defeat for the Scots must have been apparent. Leslie was taken prisoner after the English victory. Cromwell said that the fight, that had lasted for four or five hours, was one of the most arduous he had seen. Two days previously, one of his generals, George Monk, who had been in Scotland with 5000 men, had stormed and sacked Dundee.

1658

Trade continued between both countries though the Scots got little of their own way but 'were treated, on the whole, justly and kindly'. They were divided amongst themselves and Cromwell pacified them, interfering only when essential, until he died on *3 September*.

1660

Charles II's restoration on *29 May* was received with joy and the Scots were loyal subjects. Charles, however, was not loyal to them regarding the trade that affected Scotland. Thus, when the Scots sent Sharp to London to secure the settlement of Presbyterianism, Charles bought him off with the Bishopric of St Andrews.

1661

Argyll went to London to pay homage to the King. For his loyalty he was arrested and sent back to Scotland where on *27 May* he was beheaded for treason. James Guthrie, a Presbyterian minister, met a similar fate, as did Johnston of Warriston, one of the most able of the Covenanters, soon after. Charles II was crowned again at Westminster on *23 April*.

1662

An Act was passed that whoever held a public office must abjure the Covenant and that all clergy were to be confirmed by bishops. About 350 ministers who refused to comply were expelled from their parishes under the order that they must not reside within 20 miles of them, six miles of any cathedral town, or three miles from a royal burgh. Soldiers were sent to enforce the laws and deliver penalties. The people followed their ministers and held services in the hills that were soon declared illegal. The Presbyterians were so harassed and oppressed that they were driven to insurrection. Some began by disarming soldiers, making themselves doomed men. Knowing they were, they resolved to go further until they captured Sir James Turner, a captain at Dumfries, with a considerable amount of money he had collected as fines. The insurgents roused the district to their aid and, under Colonel Wallace, they marched towards Edinburgh. However, they were met at Rullion Green by General Dalziel and his troops who defeated them.

1665

The Jews did not begin settling in Scotland until around this time and it was in this year that a 'converted' Jew was given a post in Edinburgh as a teacher of oriental languages. For Jews in Scotland enjoyed a liberty unknown elsewhere at the time.

1676

More severe laws were passed against the Covenanters. Penalties were enforced on those who as much as communed with them. It was a serious offence to offer them 'meat, drink, house, harbouring, or anything necessary or convenient'.

1678

To enforce these laws about 6000 Highlanders were let loose on Ayrshire and Renfrewshire to take for free whatever housing they liked for their stay. They could imprison, wound, or even kill anyone who opposed their authority. The Highlanders were regarded with dislike and distrust as it was and carrying out these orders could in no way enhance their reputation. To make matters worse, the government also removed all the town officers, though they had been appointed by the people, and replaced them with others loyal to the episcopate.

1679

Archbishop Sharp was the most zealous anti-Covenanter. He was even hated by the unscrupulous government agents who worked with him. He was regarded by the people as a Judas who had betrayed them and his Lord. He was also feared by them because of his cunning and cruelty. As assassins waited to ambush a law officer from Fife named Carmichael, infamous for his extortion and oppression, at Magus Moor on *3 May*, they were surprised to find the Archbishop's coach arrive instead. Balfour of Burley, ignoring Archbishop Sharp's pleas for mercy, killed him on the spot in front of his grieving daughter. After he had been slashed across the face, had his hand cut off, been shot and then ridden over, his skull was crushed.

Burley and Haxton — amongst the assassins but who refused to lift a hand against Sharp — with a group of Covenanters, met John Graham of Claverhouse (Bluiddy Claver'se) and his troop of bodyguards on *1 June* at Drumclog. Though inexperienced fighters, they charged and scattered the dragoons, leaving 36 dead and losing only three of their own men. Claverhouse fled from the battle.

A large army under the Duke of Monmouth was set to crush the Covenanters. The latter took their position on *22 June* at the south of Bothwell Bridge and, to their ultimate misfortune, were arguing and squabbling amongst themselves before the battle. They suffered a terrible defeat and Monmouth, pitying more than he blamed them, halted his pursuit.

About 300 were slain and 1200 taken prisoner and penned in Greyfriars Churchyard, Edinburgh. Many died of exposure and fever and those who survived were shipped as slaves to plantations in the West Indies.

1685

Charles II died on *6 February*. The Covenanters were increasingly oppressed but this only made them more zealous. When John Brown of Priesthill declined to pray for the King on the threats of soldiers, the unarmed man was shot at his doorstep in front of his wife and child by Graham of Claverhouse, who then jeered at the woman after the murder. Women as well as men were executed by the royalist forces. On *11 May* an elderly woman and a girl of 18 were tied to stakes in the narrow channel of the Bladenoch, near Wigtown, where they were drowned by the rising tide.

James II (of England) was crowned at Westminster on *23 April* as the late King had no children and his brother was next in line to the throne. He was proclaimed James VII at Edinburgh Cross though he was a Catholic. There was an uprising in England in favour of Monmouth, illegitimate son of Charles, to take the throne because he was a Protestant. The Earl of Argyll made an attempt to back him in Scotland. He was soon captured, at Inchinnan, then sent to Edinburgh where, on *30 June*, he was beheaded for treason.

1686

Allan Ramsay, son of a mine manager at Leadhills, Lanarkshire, was born on *15 October*. He first won great fame in his day as a poet, through writing verses published by Edinburgh's Easy Club – an association of Jacobites – especially an 'Elegy on Maggy Johnston' (who was supposedly a woman of low character).

1688

Persecutions against the Presbyterians went on for some time but came to an end with the execution of James Renwick, a Cameronian minister. He was executed on *17 February*, three days after his 26th birthday.

William of Orange landed at Torbay, backed by 1400 Dutch bayonets, on *5 November*. He was a grandson of Charles II and brother-in-law of James VII who had fled the country. The English parliament, unwilling to assert that a sovereign might be deposed, claimed that James had abdicated his throne by his flight. They accepted William and Mary and demanded that the clergy proclaim the fact from the pulpit and pray for the new sovereigns. Few members of the Estates made any protest though they must have been worried, for many had joined in the previous tyranny. About 200 episcopal clergymen gave up their livings rather than conform to the new order.

1689

Parliament declared William and Mary joint sovereigns so that when one died the other was to continue ruling alone. They were crowned at Westminster on *11 April*.

The Duke of Gordon, who had been holding Edinburgh for James, had to surrender it for lack of supplies. Graham of Claverhouse, now Viscount Dundee, escaped from Edinburgh with 50 troopers to Inverness. There he met MacDonald of Keppoch about to pillage the town and won him to James' side although James, when on the throne, had issued letters of 'fire and sword' against him. As Argyll had been restored, Dundee was able to get other enemies of the Campbells – MacDonalds, Camerons and MacLeans – to join James' cause.

With these men, Viscount Dundee stationed himself at the Pass of Killiecrankie in Perthshire where, at about 7 o'clock in the evening of *27 July*, they charged General MacKay's troops who were on a march to Atholl. They were defeated before they could fasten their bayonets. MacKay did manage to rally two regiments and got them through the pass and into Stirling the following day. Dundee fell in the battle whilst signalling a charge.

On *3 July* MacKay defeated the Stuart supporters near Perth, with the loss of only one man. Cannon, Dundee's successor, advanced on Dunkeld on *21 August* with over 4000 Highlanders. The Cameronians were surrounded and their leader, Colonel Clelland, was shot dead, as was his second moments later. Their gunpowder was nearly finished and as they were ready to make a last stance, after burning surrounding buildings and intending to burn themselves and their enemies, the Highlanders unexpectedly withdrew to the hills. The war ended. MacKay erected Fort William and surrounded the clans by a chain of military posts.

1690

James VII had been welcomed in Dublin as King. When William sent the Duke of Schomberg to Ireland with an army, the Irish replied by flocking to Jacobite ranks and James was able to face the duke at Drogheda with a force double that of his opponent. To make matters worse for Schomberg, half of his troops were wiped out by pestilence at Dundalk.

William arrived in Ireland and met James' troops in the Boyne Valley on *1 July*. Early in the morning the English horsemen charged into the River Boyne and the Irish infantry fled in a panic. But the Irish cavalry made so gallant a stand that Schomberg fell while trying to repulse its charge. It held the English in check for a while. James, who had been trying to withdraw his troops rather than meet William's onset, eventually forsook his troops and fled to Kinsale. There he sailed for France, making the Stuart defeat a certainty.

1691

William of Orange had offered a pardon to those Highland chiefs who would swear before *31 December* an oath to live peaceably – in other words, to renounce their allegiance to James for that of William. The oath was taken but, proud as the chiefs were, each wished to take it *after* his neighbour. MacEoin, chief of the Glencoe MacDonalds, delayed to the last minute to preserve his dignity.

When the old chief reached Fort William, after struggling to get there through a blizzard, he found no-one there who could administer the oath. Colonel Hill gave him a letter to the sheriff at Inveraray.

1692

MacEoin hastened over the hills, not even staying at his own glen, to Inveraray, reaching it on *6 January*. Though it was past the time, the oath was administered. The two Campbell chiefs at Inveraray must have been delighted to find the MacDonalds in trouble, but Lord Stair was more merciless than they. He suppressed the certificate of the oath and procured a letter from the King ordering 'fire and sword' against the Glencoe MacDonalds. The execution of the commission was entrusted to Colonel Hamilton who was to march into Glencoe with part of an Argyll regiment. Hamilton sent Campbell of Glenlyon, whose niece was married to MacEoin's son, with 120 soldiers into Glencoe. Though their arrival created alarm, they assured peace and goodwill and so were treated to twelve days of Highland hospitality by a poor clan that could hardly support itself.

After checking all the exits from Glencoe the Campbell soldiers reported to Hamilton who fixed the morning of *13 February* for the fatal blow. The cowardly massacre was not the success the King and the government hoped for: only about 40 of the intended victims were murdered. Hamilton, with the main force, did not arrive in time to block all the exits. Surprisingly, the fierce blizzards only killed a few of those who had escaped.

In the first Scots parliament that met after the massacre, no mention of it was made.

1694

Mary II died at the end of the year. Although historians have declared that there is no cause for posterity to take much notice of her, she was a dutiful, loving and loyal wife to a cold, indifferent and insulting husband. Perhaps it was this behaviour towards his wife that has caused some to claim that William was a homosexual. She was the last of the Stuarts to sit on the throne, though William himself had Stuart blood. Her death also weakened his rule.

1695

The Darien colony was founded, as was the Bank of Scotland, on *1 November* by Scotsman William Paterson, who also founded the Bank of England. Noting that nations built on islands and swamps had drawn great wealth from the seas, he reasoned that Scotland could do likewise. His idea was that Scotland would claim as a colony the Isthmus of Darien, between Panama and Columbia, from where they would trade. He captivated the government by glowing reports of the place. An Act of Parliament was sanctioned by the Lord High Commissioner forming the Company of Scotland for trading with Africa and the Indies. A capital of £220000 in shares of £100 was raised. Edinburgh, Glasgow and Perth Corporations bought 80 between them. Paterson could have had more backing but for the jealousy of English merchants. William took their side, causing Dutch merchants to withdraw from the scheme, crippling it by the loss of half a million pounds.

1696

The Estates declared that every parish should provide a school house and pay a wage to the master. It was the first system of national education in the world. The sons of lairds, farmers and cotters (peasants who gave labour in return for their abode), were taught in the same class, many of whom remained friends throughout adulthood.

Church of Scotland ministers were extremely intolerant of the slightest difference in theological thought from theirs. It was through their instigation of a trial, from a statute reaffirmed the previous year, that Thomas Aikenhead was cruelly executed for blasphemy. The young divinity student's execution was to be the last in Scotland for the crime of blasphemy.

1698

Five ships sailed for Darien with 1200 men and settled on the isthsmus peninsula that they called New Caledonia. The tropical sun and unsuitable food brought on disease and the colonisers fled, taking to sea in ships. four hundred of them died on board.

A second expedition of four ships containing 1300 men was sent but they fared even worse. They quarrelled among themselves and a Spanish force compelled them to leave. Two of their ships were lost at sea and some of the others took jobs on plantations in Jamaica. Few ever saw Scotland again. Paterson, due to the failure of the scheme, had some kind of a nervous breakdown. When he had recovered, he went into retirement.

1700

James MacPherson, the notorious freebooter and robber, and hero of Robert Burns' song 'MacPherson's Farewell', was executed. He was hanged at Banff Mercat

Cross, not at Inverness as Sir Walter Scott averred, on *8 November*. It was the last hanging in Scotland under the Heritable Jurisdiction System.

1702

To the delight of many in Scotland, William of Orange fell off his horse when it stumbled on a molehill, causing the King to die, on *8 March*. The Jacobites especially toasted 'the little gentleman in the velvet jacket', in other words, the mole.

William was succeeded by Anne, the second daughter of James. The English parliament excluded from the throne all descendants of Charles I and chose, instead, as Anne's successor, Sophia, electress of Hanover. This choice was rejected by the Scots, causing further emnity between the countries. Anne was, however, crowned at Westminster on *3 April*.

1706

The English had proposed that there should be one kingdom, 'by the name of Great Britain', and one order of succession to the throne. The Scots eventually agreed to it but only on condition that the trade and citizenship of each country should be free to the other. The English then proposed that the new kingdom should have the same customs and excise duties, regulations of trade, money, weights and measures. The articles of an incorporating union, signed by 26 Scots commissioners and 27 English, were presented to the Queen.

There was great hostility towards the Union as never before and this was not only from the Jacobite quarter. The articles of the treaty were burned at Dumfries and the army had to quell mobs in Edinburgh and Glasgow. It was rumoured that an incongruous combination of Jacobites and Cameronians were forming a rebellion. Though the government was willing to tackle it, it did not happen.

The treaty was at last carried on *16 October* by a majority of 110 to 69.

1707

The Union of Scotland and England was proclaimed on *1 May* 1707.

1708

The Scots, in effect, had lost their own government and their representatives in parliament, due to smallness of numbers, had little influence. They became extremely dissatisfied and some families stood behind 'the Pretender' calling him James VIII of Scotland and James III of England.

He appeared off the coast of Montrose with 4000 men, with Admiral Fourbin's fleet. They reappeared later in the Forth only to flee from the ships of Admiral Bynd, who was himself later shot for failing to carry out orders.

1711

David Hume, the great philosopher who had a profound influence on European thought and is said to have awakened the German philosopher Immanuel Kant (also of Scottish descent) 'from his dogmatic slumber', was born in Edinburgh on *26 April*.

1712

A motion in the House of Lords to repeal the Union was lost by only three proxy votes. Contrary to the spirit of the Union, Church patronage was restored and the privileges of the people and the Church in the settlement of ministers was curtailed. It was mainly the cause of three subsequent secessions from the Church.

1714

Queen Anne died and, in accordance with the settlement of 1701, the elector, a great-grandson of James VI, was crowned as George I. Anne was the first sovereign to see a daily newspaper and the establishment of the GPO and the last to preside at a meeting of the Privy Council and to refuse assent to a parliamentary bill.

George I, welcomed enthusiastically by the Whigs, was regarded indifferently by the people and with hostility by the Jacobites; he was crowned at Westminster on *20 October* although he was a non-English-speaking German who preferred his own country to Britain.

1715

The Earl of Mar, after having made 'great professions of service' to George I, raised the standard of rebellion at Braemar on *6 September*. He assembled a number of Jacobites from both sides of the Grampians and James VIII was soon proclaimed in all the chief towns. Twelve thousand men rallied to the cause; the government did not have 2000 troops in Scotland.

Mar's forces marched to Preston on *13 November*, where they were attacked by the royal troops and eventually surrendered. James landed with six followers at Peterhead on *22 December*.

Sir John Clerk of Penicuik started a tradition among the Scottish upper classes by sending his son to Eton. Since then many Scottish nobles have done likewise, creating a chasm between the anglicised aristocracy and the rest of Scottish society that had not previously existed.

1716

Because of James' defeatist attitude, that many of his followers regarded as unkingly, much of his army dispersed. James sailed from Montrose to France, accompanied by Mar, on *3 February*. About 20 people were executed for their part in the rebellion, and 40 high-ranking Scottish families had their estates confiscated, while many became exiles for life.

1721

The first games of golf in Scotland are reported having been played on Glasgow Green, though acts against the game in the 15th century would imply that it was being played then by ordinary people – as it was definitely a sport of the monarchs since James IV's time.

1724

There were big crowds attending a golf match in Leith – between Alexander Elphinstone, younger son of Lord Balmerino, and Captain John Porteous of the town guard. They played for a stake of 20 guineas.

1725

There had been discontent in Scotland over high taxation, especially regarding malt. The military were needed to quell a riot that broke out in Glasgow because the mob believed the Provost had acted as an informer. Several military roads were constructed in the Highlands by General Wade. Fort Augustus was erected in Glenmore and another garrison at Inverness.

Allan Ramsay, the poet, was also a pioneer in the book trade, with successful shops in Edinburgh's Grassmarket, the High Street and the luckenbooths. It was during this year that he founded the first circulating library in Scotland and the whole of Britain.

1727

The Royal Bank of Scotland was instituted, in addition to the Bank of Scotland, the latter being founded in 1695. Business in Scotland also saw the constitution of the Board of Manufacturers. George I, who had inspired a Jacobite rebellion and an assassination attempt on his life, died finally of apoplexy in his much beloved Hanover, not to any regret of either his English or his Scottish subjects. His son, though essentially a German, a Whig and a soldier, was not as unpopular as his father, despite his notorious immorality. He was crowned at Westminster on *11 October*.

It was during this year in *June* that the last witch was executed in Scotland. Janet Horne was brought before Captain David Ross, deputy-sheriff of Sutherland, at Dornoch charged with witchcraft and consorting with the devil. She was accused of 'Horse and Hattock', in other words, helping the devil to shod her daughter with horseshoes. As her daughter was lame, it was proof enough for Ross who convicted her. Her punishment was execution by being put in a tar barrel that was then set alight.

1732

The Rev Ebeneezer Erskine of Stirling preached a sermon denouncing recent legislation made by the Church of Scotland that forced congregations to accept unwanted ministers. He and three of his followers were deposed the following year.

1734

Rob Roy MacGregor died, aged about 74 on *28 December*. He was immortalised by Sir Walter Scott, although a legend in his own lifetime, but might have been neither were he not cheated by a friend and, penniless and desperate, he was forced to become a bandit and the equivalent of today's 'protection' racketeers.

1736

Two notorious smugglers, Wilson and Robertson, were imprisoned in the Tolbooth awaiting execution for having robbed a tax collector. Wilson helped his accomplice to escape while unable to do so himself. His self-sacrifice won the admiration of the mob who, on the day of his execution, rioted in his support. History records the incident as the Porteous Riots, as Captain Porteous was the leader of the town guard. When the mob pelted them, the guard replied by opening fire and killing several people. Porteous was tried and condemned to death. A reprieve was granted to allow time for an inquiry but the mob, afraid that he would be acquitted, broke into the Tolbooth and dragged the captain to the Mercat Cross where they hanged him.

James Watt, the famous engineer and inventor was born at Greenock on *19 January*. He was the hero of the popular myth that he invented the steam engine by playing with a spoon on a kettle lid.

1739

The Black Watch, otherwise known as the 42nd regiment, was founded. Prior to its establishment as a proper regiment, it had been employed by the government to act as a force to police the Highlands.

1744

The Honourable Company of Edinburgh Golfers was founded. It is reckoned to be the world's first golf club. They competed for a silver club, presented by the City of Edinburgh. John Rattray, a surgeon, won the cup. It was during that year when the first (13) rules of the game were drawn up. It was known as 'the Leith Code'.

1745

After sailing from St Nazaire on the Loire, on *22 June*, 'Bonnie Prince Charlie' landed on the west coast of Inverness-shire. On *19 August* he raised his standard at Glenfinnan, west of Lochiel, among his Cameronian and other followers who numbered 1500. Sir John Cope, commander of the government forces in Scotland, marched north to meet him. Turning off towards Inverness, he left the main Highland road open to Charles, who entered Perth on *4 September*. On the *5 September* he took Edinburgh and held court at Holyrood.

On *22 September*, the Prince, with the generalship of Lord George Murray, met Cope's troops at Prestonpans and, outnumbering them 3000 to 2000, utterly routed them. The victory also won the Prince money and reinforcements, enabling the 'Young Pretender' to march south with 6000 men.

On *18 November* his men reached Carlisle. From there they marched through Cumberland, Westmorland and Lancashire and Cheshire, reaching Derby on *14 December*. The English Jacobites did not come to their aid and Charles' men were now being opposed by three armies, each of 10000 men. A retreat was imperative. Once back in Scotland they levied contributions on Dumfries and Glasgow and besieged Stirling Castle where their numbers were increased to 9000.

1746

The English general, General Hawley attacked Charles at Falkirk on *17 January* but was forced to retreat. The Duke of Cumberland's advance, however, caused the Jacobites to retreat from Stirling and Crieff. One group marched to Inverness via Blair Atholl and the other via Aberdeen.

The war came to an end on *16 April* at Culloden Moor, where Cumberland completely defeated the Jacobites. The lords Balmerino, Kilmarnock and Lovat, who had been Jacobite leaders, were executed, as were many others, for treason. After spending time as a fugitive on the Western Isles, Charles at last made his escape in a French vessel, *L'Heureux*, and landed at Morlaix on *29 September*. Fort George was erected near Inverness to check any further rising of Highland clans.

1747

Since the Church at this time was 'on the defensive,' there was a demand for secularised schools known as 'writing' or 'commercial' schools. Their subject emphasis was on arithmetic and book-keeping. The first one in Scotland opened in Dumfries and it remained the only one for 24 years until another was opened at Stirling.

1748

Hereditary sheriffdoms were abolished. These sheriff-doms gave the barons' courts as much power as the kings'. Those on their lands could be ordered by their lords into military service. Regular circuits were from then on made by the King's courts.

1752

Rev Thomas Gillespie of Carnock founded the Relief Church in opposition to the Church of Scotland legislation that a minister could be appointed against the will of the congregation.

The Glasgow University printer, Robert Foulis, made a premature, if not naïve, attempt at trying to establish a Scottish Academy of Art. Scotland, at that time, had produced little in the way of eminent painters or sculptors (excluding the early Celtic artists), as the few who were successful were to be found abroad.

The Reformation in Scotland was a death blow to artistic aspiration, for, unlike the Netherlands where it also took root, Scotland did not have the rich guilds to commission artists such as those who commissioned Rembrandt for example. Though Foulis' attempt failed, his venture did at least produce one painter of talent – David Allan, who started a tradition of domestic genre pictures that were distintively Scottish.

1754

William Murdock, engineer and inventor of coal gas lighting in 1795, was born at Auchinleck in Ayrshire, on *21 August.*

The great architect Robert Adam, designer of Edinburgh's Register House, Dundee's former town house and Culzean Castle, set off on his grand tour of Europe. His studies in France (under Clerisseau) and Italy, where he was influenced by the graphics of Piranesi, were to shape his development as an architect. Little is known of his life before he made the tour, other than that he matriculated at Edinburgh University in 1743.

The Royal and Ancient Golf Club at St Andrews was founded. Twenty-two noblemen and others of Fife competed for a silver club. It was won by Baillie William Laudale, a St Andrews merchant.

1760

George II died and his reign is best remembered for seeing the last of the Jacobite uprisings. He has the distinction of being the last British King to lead his troops into a battle they won.

James MacPherson made his first literary mark by publishing in Edinburgh his *Fragments of Ancient Poetry*. He had published a poem two years before called *The Highlander* but it did not attract any notice as it only showed 'his ambition and incompetence' and is not regarded as having any literary merit. *The Fragments* opened the door to fame for him.

1770

The Clyde Trust was created. It converted a small ford-able stream into one of the greatest shipping emporiums in the world. A massive programme of excavation and dredging enabled the Clyde, formerly an insignificant river, to compete with the Thames and the Mersey in maritime communications.

1771

Sir Walter Scott was born on *15 August* at Edinburgh.

Mungo Park was born, the seventh of 13 children, at Foulshiels near Selkirk on *10 September*. From an early age he showed much progress as a scholar 'not so much by his ready talents, as by his remarkable perseverence and application'. He was to become a surgeon and an eminent explorer in West Africa.

1774

Robert Fergusson, 'the poetical Jan Steen of the old town of Edinburgh', died in a madhouse on *16 October* at the age of 24. He had a severe illness that started in January and caused him to sink into a religious melancholia. He was betrayed into entering the madhouse by friends. He was buried in the Canongate churchyard, largely forgotten by the people of Edinburgh, and still is. Burns erected, at his own expense some 15 years later, a memorial stone in the graveyard. Fergusson's death actually brought about a reformation regarding the treatment of the mentally ill in Scotland.

1761

James MacPherson's *Fingal* was published, the first of his 'Ossianic' legends that became a controversy from the outset. Although his skills as a translator were considered fraudulent, his prowess as a poet is undeni-able. His 'Ossianic' translations, or frauds, led to a rise in Romanticism. Napoleon claimed he slept with a copy of *Fingal* and Goethe claimed he had forsaken reading Homer for MacPherson!

Due to the reaction against the classics as recognised education, and the need for it to meet the rapid growth of commerce, the academies were founded. The first was Perth Academy and the pupils received all their lessons in English. They were independent of the town councils as their upkeep was paid for by fees.

1776

Adam Smith, son of a Kirkcaldy Comptroller of Customs, wrote and published his famous *The Wealth of Nations*. During the same year he left Edinburgh for London where he joined a club frequented by Joshua Reynolds, David Garrick and Samuel Johnson. This departure happened soon after the death of his close friend, David Hume. Hume died 'with great composure' on *25 August* and was buried at Edinburgh's Calton Hill cemetery. His writings could not have been very popular at that time because a hostile crowd gathered at his funeral and the grave had to be watched for eight nights.

1783

Glasgow saw its first newspaper. It was a weekly but changed to a daily in 1805 when it became the *Glasgow Herald*.

1784

The Highland and Agricultural Society was established, the same year as the Scottish Fishery Board.

1786

The Commission for Northern Lighthouses was established. Kilmarnock published Robert Burns' *Poems Chiefly in the Scottish Dialect*.

1788

The old Saracen's Head inn in Glasgow's Gallowgate was the first, and Scotland's chief, coaching station. It had stables for 60 horses. The first London–Glasgow mail coach reached it on *7 July*.

1790

The Jacobite heroine, Flora Macdonald, who helped 'Bonnie Prince Charlie' escape from the government forces to the Hebridean island of Benbecula, died on *5 March*. Although there was a price on the Prince's head of £30000 she, with many other Highlanders who knew of his whereabouts, remained loyal. She paid for her loyalty with imprisonment. After spending much of her life in Canada, she returned to Skye where she died.

1792

Cotton spinning was introduced into Glasgow. Within a few decades the city had become an important cotton centre and many spinning and weaving mills were erected.

1796

A barrister, whose life was more devoted to the study of German poetry and romance than the legal profession, published his first writings, a translation of Burgher's *Leonore* and *Der Wilde Jagger*. It was not a particularly successful venture, though he was to become known to the world as Sir Walter Scott, one of our most distinguished novelists and poets.

Robert Burns died on *27 July* aged 37 at Dumfries and was buried there.

1799

Lord Braxfield, 'the Judge Jeffries of Scotland', died. He denied basic rights to all but the rich, telling one accused man, 'you'd be nane the waur for a hinging'. Few indeed lamented this severe, dour man's death.

Thomas Campbell, author of 'Ye Mariners of England' and other famous and popular ballads, published his 'Pleasures of Hope'.

1802

Robert Chambers, bookseller and founder of the famous publishing house, was born on *10 July* at Peebles.

The *Edinburgh Review*, published by Archibald Constable and edited by Frances Jeffrey, first appeared in October. Jeffrey was later to be elected as rector of Glasgow University. This was an active time for publishing in Scotland: the *Dundee Advertiser*, Dundee's first newspaper, appeared a year before, while the *Aberdeen Chronicle*, Aberdeen's first, appeared four years later.

1803

'The Mountain Bard', the first of James Hogg's early scattered poems, was published, introducing his name to the literary world. He was discovered by Walter Scott, who took him under his wing.

1804

One of the most famous works of the great engineer, Thomas Telford, was begun: the Caledonian Canal. It took 18 years to complete and proved to be a white elephant. Its position in the hills made it particularly vulnerable to the winds, rendering it useless for sailing ships and, due to the high charges levied, steam-ships preferred the long voyages around the coastline instead.

After a stroke of apoplexy, Adam, Lord Duncan, Admiral of the White and British naval hero, returned to his native Scotland. He died at Cornhill near Kelso soon after, on *4 August*, on his way home to Lundie in the Carse of Gowrie. He is buried in the family vault at Lundie churchyard.

1810

The first savings banks were founded, giving the working classes access to banking their money. They were the brainchild of the Rev H Duncan of Ruthwell. They proved to be popular. By 1874 their deposits amounted to £5 million – an amazing sum for that time.

1812

The *Comet*, built by Henry Bell, was launched on the Clyde. It was the first steamboat on a navigable river and the Clyde soon became the world's greatest name in steam shipbuilding.

1814

This was the year when Walter Scott published *Waverley* and launched his career as a popular novelist.

1819

One of Dundee's most remarkable worthies, David Watson, died on *12 February* in the poor area of Hawkhill. He was remarkably fit and possessed all of his faculties till his dying day, being 102 when he died. He fathered 23 children, many of whose descendants still reside in the Dundee area.

1821

Irvine-born John Galt wrote and published his first political satire, *The Annals of the Parish*, recognised today as a classic. Coleridge claimed of his writing: 'I know of no equal in our language.'

John Rennie, a Scottish engineer and well-known designer of bridges, died on *4 October* in London.

1822

Sir Henry Raeburn, the fashionable portrait painter, who, it was said, often fell in love with his subjects, was knighted at Hopetoun House. 'The Scottish Reynolds', as he has been called, would have been made a baronet by the King, George IV. The King is supposed to have said to Walter Scott that he would have been 'but for the slur on the memory of Reynolds'. He knighted Raeburn while on a famous visit to Scotland. It was the first royal visit to the country since the time of Charles II.

1823

David Wilkie, later Sir, succeeded Raeburn, his superior in that field, as the King's Limner in Scotland.

This was the same year that the chemist Charles Macintosh developed and patented the waterproof fabric that was to bear his name.

1824

Edinburgh Academy was founded as a reaction against anti-classical education in Scotland. It could also be said to be a reaction against the egalitarian nature of traditional Scottish education as one of its functions was to educate 'a better class of boy'.

1826

Though small railways had been used for the coal and iron industries, the first proper commercial railway opened. It was the Dalkeith and Edinburgh. But it was not fully mechanised until 19 years later. The

Monkland and Kirkintilloch also opened in 1826 and was to become a more important line.

1828

James Neilson invented the hot blast oven and introduced it to industries in Glasgow for their furnaces. It was a great boon to the iron industry in Scotland which itself prospered because of the thriving coal industry in Ayrshire, Fife and Lanarkshire.

1832

The Reform Act increased Scotland's Members of Parliament to 53 and also gave the vote to those in burghs paying annual rents of £10 and those in counties paying £50.

Sir Walter Scott died at Abbotsford on *21 September* and was buried at Dryburgh Abbey.

1833

The Municipal Reform Act gave voters in burghs the right to elect town councillors and choose magistrates. Jute was introduced into Scotland, taking over from flax as it was cheaper.

Annandale-born Thomas Carlyle, one of the greatest moral forces in Britain at the time, moved to London with his wife, leaving their farm in Dumfriesshire. The same year he published *Sartor Resartus*. Though he was to remain in London for the rest of his life, living at Cheyne Walk and earning the appellation of 'the sage of Chelsea', he remained a Scot at heart.

1835

Hugh Miller was certainly a 'lad o' pairts'. Almost entirely self-educated, this Cromarty stonemason, an excellent craftsman, became a journalist and leading writer of his day. He was, for a time, editor of the *Witness*, a newspaper published by the Church of Scotland's independent wing. He was passionately interested in geology, writing a great deal on the subject, convinced that it was not incompatible with the biblical account of creation. However, he came under great mental stress and eventually, on *23 December*, shot himself.

1837

Madeleine Smith, a young Glasgow heiress, walked free from the Glasgow law courts on *9 July* having been acquitted of murder after a nine-day trial. She had murdered her lover, Pierre L'Angelier, a penniless Channel Islander. History has proved her, without a doubt, to have committed the murder though her judges, obviously, wilfully disregarded the evidence against her. The decision to acquit her has been seen, in retrospect, as one where the interests of the ruling class were protected by the judges, themselves members of the peerage. They would not admit evidence to be shown that would have proved Miss Smith had poisoned her lover. The case made daily headlines.

David Livingston, after studying for a year at Glasgow's Anderton College, left Scotland for London to join the Missionary Society. Four years later it was to send him to Africa where he was to become renowned as an explorer and one of the most famous men of his time.

1842

Sir James Dewar, physicist and chemist, best known as the inventor of the vacuum flask, was born in Kincardine, Fife on *20 September*.

1843

On account of disputes arising chiefly from the Law of Patronage, 474 ministers left the Church of Scotland and formed the Free Church.

1845

A poor law gave powers to the parish boards throughout Scotland to care for the poor. It also permitted them to levy rates for their maintenance.

1846

In 'recognition of his exertions in procuring an acceleration of the mail', Dundonian James Chalmers, supposed inventor of the adhesive postage stamp, received on *1 January* a silver plate and a sum of money (both of which came to the value of £200). When the government offered £200 for the best plan of a postage token, over 2000 people came up with the same idea as Chalmers and that is why, although the idea was taken up, the £200 was never paid out.

1850

Robert Louis Stevenson, author of *Treasure Island* and *Kidnapped*, was born at 8 Howard Place, Edinburgh on *13 November*. He was the son and grandson of famous lighthouse builders.

1855

Queen Victoria and Prince Albert had Balmoral Castle built, largely to a design made by the Prince himself. It started a fashion and rich landowners copied the example, building castles in the Scottish baronial style. It was about this time when 'Scotland became respectable' – due to the Royal couple becoming patrons of the romantic artist, Sir Edwin Landseer. Landseer painted many Scottish scenes that included wildlife. His most famous is the *Monarch of the Glen*.

1857

From this year onwards each Scottish county and burgh had to fall in with England and provide a police force. (The first in England were set up by Sir Robert Peel in 1829.)

1859

Kenneth Graham, Scottish author who is best known for *The Wind in the Willows* was born in Edinburgh on *8 March*.

1860

The world's first professional golf tournament was held at Prestwick on *17 October*; it was won by Willie Park.

1861

The first British golf open was played at Prestwick on *26 September*; it was won by Tom Morris.

1865

The last public execution in Britain took place in Glasgow on *28 July*: Dr Edward William Pritchard was hanged for the murder of his mother-in-law and his wife. He also murdered at least one of his mistresses and was as notorious a liar as he was a philanderer. He was not a successful doctor, being quite openly despised by his fellow practitioners in the city, but shamelessly lived off his wife, whose money he squandered.

1868

The growth in collective bargaining fostered the co-operative movement, culminating in the formation of the Scottish Co-Operative Wholesale Society. The SCWS, nicknamed the 'Sosh' by their mainly working-class clientele, also ran jute mills. Their stores, in effect, were the forerunners of today's supermarkets. They were popular because they kept their prices low by buying in bulk. They paid back their profits to the shoppers by way of dividends. The idea of 'co-ops' came from the mind of the man who also came up with the idea of trades unions – Robert Owen of New Lanark.

1869

The famous tea ship or 'clipper' the *Cutty Sark*, which was the last of the fast sailing ships and capable of moving at a speed of 17½ knots, was built by Scott and Linton of Dumbarton and launched there.

1870

Sir Harry Lauder, one of the greatest and foremost comic singers and music hall entertainers of all time, was born at Portobello, near Edinburgh, on *4 August*.

William McTaggart, the Campbeltown-born artist whom it has been said was painting Impressionist pictures ten years before the term was first coined, gained RSA status that year. Much of his work portrayed the 'innocent mirth of child life, finding vent for itself amidst bright sunshine and happy associations'.

1871

The idea of chain stores probably originated with two Glasgow grocers, Marcus Lipton and Thomas Bishop, who founded two of the first, Lipton's and Cooper's. Lipton opened his first shop in 1871 and Bishop opened his the same year, calling it Cooper's. Bishop's shops were advanced for the time; his shop in Sauchiehall Street was the first in Scotland to have electric lighting.

The first real Rugby Union international took place in Edinburgh on *27 March* at Raeburn Place; the ground was controlled by the Edinburgh Academical Cricket Club Committee. (The first ever Scotland versus England Rugby Union international was played in the November of 1870 but the majority of the 'Scottish' players had very tenuous links with Scotland indeed!)

Though there was no scoring by half-time in the Raeburn Place match, A Buchan scored a goal then R H Birket scored a try as did W Cross. So Scotland won by a goal and two tries to nil.

1872

The first British international soccer tournament took place between Scotland and England on *30 November* at Glasgow. The game resulted in an 0–0 draw.

1873

The Scottish Football Association was founded on *13 March* by a meeting of the representatives of eight clubs. Rangers Football Club was also formed that year in Glasgow.

1876

Alexander Graham Bell, a native of Edinburgh, transmitted his first coherent statement on a telephone on *10 March*. He spoke to his assistant in their offices in Massachusetts, saying, 'Come here, Watson. I want you.'

As he beat Elisha Gray, who had invented a similar machine, to filing for a patent by only three hours, Bell may not have been the first to make a clear statement on the phone. However, history has credited him with inventing the telephone and not Gray.

The first Scotland versus Wales international took place in Glasgow on *25 March*. Scotland won 5–0.

1877

The worst mining disaster in Scotland's history happened at Blantyre near Hamilton on *22 October* when 220 men were killed in an explosion there. Due to the disaster, almost every family with a male member in the small country town suffered a bereavement.

1879

William Denny of Dumbarton built and launched the first steel-hulled ocean-going vessel.

Blantyre saw its second pit disaster on *2 July* in which 26 men were killed.

The Tay Railway Bridge, then the longest railway bridge in the world, from Wormit to Dundee, designed by Thomas Bouch, collapsed in a severe gale on *28 December*. The Edinburgh to Dundee train was on it at the time with all its staff and passengers – many of whom were intending to celebrate Hogmanay. The exact number of people killed in the disaster is not known and reports vary from 90 to over 300.

1881

A university college was founded in Dundee to be incorporated in St Andrews University.

1883

The Boys' Brigade was founded in Glasgow on *4 October* by Sir William Alexander Smith.

After much travelling abroad and marriage in California, Robert Louis Stevenson returned to Scotland where he wrote his first successful novel, *Treasure Island*. It was published the same year, bringing him instant fame.

1884

The first Ireland versus Scotland soccer international took place in Belfast on *28 January*. The guests beat the hosts 5–0.

1885

The record victory recorded in any British – probably world! – soccer cup tie took place on *12 September* at Arbroath. The final result was Arbroath 36, Bon Accord 0.

1888

Celtic Park opened in the Parkhead area of Glasgow on *8 May* with the match between Hibs and Cowlairs ending in a goalless draw. The same day Queen Victoria opened the Glasgow Exhibition of Industry, Science and Art at Kelvingrove.

On Monday *28 May* Celtic played their first major game. It was the first Glasgow 'old firm' between Celtic and Rangers. Though Rangers were the more experienced side, having been established for 15 years, Celtic beat them 5–0. The game took place in front of 2000 spectators.

John Logie Baird, who pioneered, and is credited with inventing television, was born at Helensburgh on *13 August*.

1890

The spectacular Forth Rail Bridge, a 1710-foot cantilever bridge, was officially opened by the Prince of Wales, later Edward VIII. The longest in Britain, its total length, including the approach viaducts, is 2916 feet. It took 5000 men to build it over a period of six years and at a cost of £3 177 206 (the present-day estimate would be over £40 million) and 57 were killed during its construction. It was designed and constructed by Sir Benjamin Baker and Sir John Fowler and the contractor was Sir William Arrol, a man who achieved a tremendous amount in his lifetime. (Sir William was born into a very poor family in 1839 at Houston, Renfrewshire, where he was forced to work in a thread factory at the age of nine. Apprenticed to a blacksmith in his early teens, he then became a boiler-maker and eventually went into iron-working on a large scale and became the engineer for the second Tay Bridge.)

1892

The renowned scientist, William Thomson, inventor and Professor of Mathematics and Natural Philosophy (a chair he was appointed to when he was only 22 years old) and exponent of two of the Laws of Thermodynamics, was created Lord Kelvin of Largs. Though Irish by birth, he saw himself as a Scot as he spent most of his life in Scotland, worked in Scotland and was of Scots ancestry.

1895

Celtic had their record win of all time when they defeated Dundee 11–0 on *26 October*.

That same year the first Scottish motor car was built and on sale to the general public. This car, the Arrol-Johnston, did a top speed of 17 mph and its manufacturer, Johnston, was actually fined for speeding! These contraptions were often called 'horseless carriages' because they resembled uncovered traps.

1896

Glasgow underground railway opened on *14 December*, the first, and to remain the only, one in Scotland. It was worked by cable until it was electrified in 1935.

1897

Scotland led the way in the trades unions movements, forming the STUC. It played a significant, if not a major, part in the Scottish Works Parliamentary Committee three years later.

Work began on the Glasgow Art School in Renfrew Street, just off Sauchiehall Street. Considered to be a masterpiece it was created by the Art Nouveau architect Charles Rennie Mackintosh. Though he was never given much recognition in Scotland, Mackintosh has been regarded as a genius by the world's art lovers: he was also an accomplished painter and designer.

1898

The first moving pictures were shown in Scotland when they were presented to Queen Victoria at Balmoral Castle on *24 October*. Her Majesty had seen a local cinematographic enthusiast filming at a recent Braemar gathering and, in response to a royal request, the man, William Walker, gave a command performance at Balmoral.

1900

Alastair Sim, a famous comedy actor who appeared in many of the 1950s 'Ealing Comedies' such as *The Belles of St Trinian's*, was born at Edinburgh on *9 October*.

1901

Glasgow Public Art Galleries and museum were built and opened.

1903

The multi-millionaire and philanthropist Andrew Carnegie purchased the 'Glen' of Dunfermline, his home town, for the purpose of turning it into a public park and presenting it to the people. He left Dunfermline as a penniless youth for America where he made a massive fortune. He spent £70 million of it on philanthropic enterprises.

1906

The Scottish Labour Party was founded by members of the Scottish Workers' Parliamentary Election Committee. This was the springboard for the British Labour Party as, three years later, it amalgamated with the Labour Representation Committee to become the British Labour Party. The foremost founder of the Party was Lanarkshire-born Keir Hardie.

1908

Attempts had been made to follow Balfour's 1902 Education Act in England that replaced school boards with county and borough councils. Tradition in Scotland, however, rendered such attempts null and void. Under the Education Act of 1908 the powers of the school boards in Scotland were extended. Balfour, the Prime Minister responsible for the 1902 Act, was himself a Scot – but, like the three Scottish Prime Ministers before him, he was an extremely anglicised one, having been educated at Eton and Cambridge.

1910

David Niven, film actor and Oscar winner in 1958, was born at Kirriemuir on *1 March*. He played in numerous Hollywood roles, including the part of 'Bonnie Prince Charlie', although he was known as 'the perfect Englishman'.

1911

Riots started on the morning of *18 December* in Dundee when picketing dock workers attacked jute carters who were taking jute from the docks to the mills. Even the police, 'of whom there was a strong posse', were swept aside by the mob who attacked the lorries. The riots were to continue throughout December, rallying more strikers to the cause. As tempers worsened, 60 policemen were drafted into the city from Glasgow and Edinburgh, marching through Dundee like an army battalion. But it only exacerbated the situation and about midday on *20 December*, after a fist fight with the police, the enraged mob unhitched a cab from a lorry and the latter, full of empty biscuit boxes, plunged into one of the docks. The following day the military were dispatched to Dundee to quell the mob.

1915

The worst train disaster in the United Kingdom happened at Dumfries on *22 May*. A triple collision at Quintins Hill, near Gretna Green, killed 227 people.

1917

One hundred and forty-three recipients of military honours were decorated at Ibrox Stadium, Glasgow, by the King, George V, on *18 September*. The audience cheered loudest when Corporal Henry Christian, of the Royal Lancaster Regiment, was carried on a chair by St Andrew's ambulancemen to have a VC pinned on to his chest by the sovereign. Mr Christian had collapsed prior to entering the stadium.

1918

An Education Act instigated the replacement of school boards in Scotland by elected education authorities. There was to be one authority for each county and one respectively for Aberdeen, Dundee, Edinburgh, Glasgow and Leith.

1921

Earl Haig (Douglas Haig) Commander-in-Chief of the British Army during the First World War and founder of the British Legion in 1921, died on *29 January* at London. His body was sent back to Scotland and interred in Dryburgh Abbey.

Deborah Kerr, the famous British film star who made her name in the 1940s film *From Here to Eternity* which also starred Frank Sinatra and Montgomery Clift, was born at Helensburgh on *30 September*. She also played Anna in the 1950s box-office musical hit *The King and I* in which she was Yul Brynner's co-star.

1923

Lady Elizabeth Bowes-Lyon, youngest daughter of the Earl of Strathmore and Kinghorne, married HRH the Duke of York, later King George VI on the abdication of his elder brother, Edward VIII, on *26 April*. The marriage of Lady Elizabeth to the Duke of York was to inadvertently result in her becoming the British Queen. She and her husband were crowned on *12 May* 1937.

Glasgow Corporation took over the running of the city's underground.

1924

Ramsay MacDonald, who was born in 1886 in Lossiemouth, the illegitimate son of a Scottish laird and a Morayshire girl, took office as the first Labour Prime Minister on *22 January*. He took over the running of Britain on the resignation of Stanley Baldwin.

Scotsman Eric Liddell won the Gold Medal at the Paris Olympics for running in the 400 metres. He also broke the world record at the same time – a feat that no other Scot has ever done.

1925

Hugh MacDiarmid, who was born Christopher Murray Grieve at Langholm in Dumfriesshire in 1892, published his first book of poems: *Sangschaw*. He was recognised as the foremost Scottish dialect poet of his time although he has been accused of writing synthetic Scots. His most famous poem is 'A Drunk Man Looks at the Thistle'.

1926

Helensburgh-born John Logie Baird gave the first public demonstration of television to members of the Royal Institution on *27 January* in his Soho workshop, London.

Baird, who had studied for a BSc at Glasgow University, had worked for a short time afterwards as an electrical supply engineer until bad health caused him to give it up. He then became an inventor and, by 1926, was the first man to demonstrate that television was a practical possibility. With the help of the BBC he sent moving pictures along a telephone line to one of their studios. When the BBC started the world's first

TV service a decade later, it was *not* Baird's system that they employed. Though television has been a world-wide success, for Baird, like the rest of his inventions, it was a huge flop.

Moira Shearer, ballerina and wife of fellow Scot, the writer and broadcaster Ludovic Kennedy, was born at Dunfermline on *17 January* as Moira King. The daughter of a civil engineer, she achieved international fame starring in the ballet film *The Red Shoes*. The shoes were enchanted and anyone who wore them danced themselves to death, that is except for the star of the film.

1929

The 'talkies' came to Scotland. The first one was shown in Glasgow on *7 January*. It was a 'weepy' called *The Singing Fool* and starred the great American tenor, Al Jolson. This, however, was not the first talkie to be made.

1930

The *Empress of Britain*, a luxury liner, was launched by the Prince of Wales (later Edward VIII) at Clydebank on *11 June*.

Sean Connery, star of the James Bond films in the 1960s, was born at Edinburgh as Thomas Connery on *25 August*. He first made his name in films in the early 60s playing alongside Janet Munro in the film *Darby O'Gill and the Little People*. He has starred in numerous Hollywood box-office hits since.

1931

This was the year of first publication of A J Cronin's *Hatter's Castle* that became an instant success, though the author had received many rejection slips from publishers for it. So enthusiastic was he over its popularity that he gave up a successful medical career and devoted himself to writing.

1932

The present-day Scottish National Party has its roots in a small right-wing group that broke away from the British Conservative Party because of what it saw as Tory indifference towards Scotland. The group was derived from a breakaway group of the Cathcart Unionist Association in Glasgow. They proposed 'a moderate Home Rule' and attracted the support of the Duke of Montrose, Sir Alexander MacEwan and Professor A Dewar Gibb of Glasgow University. But the radical left-wing poet Hugh MacDiarmid was also a leading founding member of what later became the SNP.

1934

The British liner, the *Queen Mary*, was launched on *2 September* at John Brown's shipyard at Clydebank. It was the world's largest liner at the time.

Rangers had their record victory in the first leg of the Scottish cup. They played Blairgowrie on *20 January* and defeated them 14–2.

1936

George Andrew McMahon, a Scottish journalist working in London, was charged at Bow Street with 'being in possession of a revolver with intent to endanger life'.

McMahon was extremely fortunate that that was all he was charged with as the life he intended to endanger was that of the King, Edward VIII! As he tried to shoot the King, during a royal parade on *16 July*, he could have been charged with high treason. An unrepentant McMahon said from the dock, 'The King was not hurt in any way, was he?'

1937

Hampden Park, Glasgow, saw its largest crowd on record; it was the record attendance for any British football game. On *17 April* 149 547 people watched Scotland play England.

Celtic faced their record defeat on *30 April* in a league game when Motherwell defeated them 8–0.

Two famous Scots also died that year: J M Barrie, the author, on *19 June* and Labour's first Prime Minister, Ramsay MacDonald, on *9 November*.

1938

The Empire Exhibition was opened in Glasgow's Bellahouston Park, in the depressed south-west area of the city, on *3 May* by King George VI and Queen

Elizabeth. This prototype of world fairs took over 3000 workers to construct and, when it had been completed, was the size of a small town. The cost was £10 million in all. As the gates opened to admit 150 000 people, Hitler was meeting Mussolini in Rome.

The *Queen Elizabeth*, the largest ocean liner ever built, was launched by the Queen Mother at Clydebank on *27 September*.

1939

Jackie Stewart, who was to become the world champion motor-car driver, was born at Milton in Dumbarton on *11 June*.

1941

Kirkintilloch-born Tom Johnston was made Secretary of State for Scotland by Sir Winston Churchill on *8 February*. Known for his distrust of the English, Johnston, a staunch socialist and one-time editor of the *Forward*, a socialist weekly, was excluded from membership of London's exclusive Caledonian Club because of his renowned pet hatred of the Scottish aristocracy. It was through Johnston that America came into the war. Harry Hopkins, President Roosevelt's aide, was in Britain trying to find out if Britain could defeat Hitler and would give no inkling whether America would come to Britain's aid. At a dinner party in the North British Hotel in Glasgow's George Square, held by Johnston for Hopkins and Winston Churchill, the Scots put the American in an embarrassing situation by asking him to make a speech. Hopkins had to say that America would back Britain in the war. By that it was taken for granted that they would become one of Britain's allies.

Rudolph Hess, 'Hitler's envoy', parachuted from a crashing Messerschmitt fighter plane near Glasgow on Saturday *10 May*. He was found, with a broken ankle, in a field by a local ploughman. The ploughman took the Nazi to his home and offered him a cup of tea. Hess declined, saying that he never drank tea at night. He said he had an important message for the Duke of Hamilton whom he met at once. Several hours later, the Germans broadcast a statement that Hess had been suffering from hallucinations. The British press said, 'he may just be a mental case.'

1943

Upwards of 200 bombers took part in the Luftwaffe's offensive on Clydebank on *Thursday, 13 March*. The first bombs fell on Clydebank at about 9.30 pm and enormous fires started as Singer's 60-acre timber-yard caught fire, as did the Yorker distillery and the admiralty's oil storage tanks at Dalnottar. Five hundred and twenty-eight people died in Clydebank alone. In Jellicoe Street all 15 members of the Rock family died in the first attack. Nearby the McSherry family, a widow and her seven children, were also wiped out. Another raid took place the following night.

In those two nights over 1000 people were killed in the Glasgow area and 439 of Hitler's Luftwaffe dropped 500 tons of high explosive and about 2500 incendiary bombs on the city.

At Dalnottar Cemetery the dead were buried in haste. Only seven houses in Clydebank were undamaged and over 50 000 people were forced to live in temporary homes and had to travel 50 or 60 miles a day to and from their work.

1942

Willie Carson, the champion jockey, was born at Stirling on *16 November*. He is best remembered for being the first jockey to the Queen in 1977. This great horseriding champion's best year was in 1979 when he won the Derby, the Irish Derby, the King George VI stakes, The Queen Elizabeth II Stakes and the Benson and Hedges Gold Cup.

1947

Lord Boyd-Orr, a leading architect of the Western Food Policies, aimed at helping starving nations, was awarded the Nobel Peace Prize. The Swedish Academy telephoned him on *12 October* to inform him of the fact. Formerly Sir John Boyd-Orr, he was director of the United Nations Food and Agricultural Organisation.

1950

Sir Harry Lauder, the great music hall comedian, who made songs like 'A Wee Doch an Dorus', 'Roamin' in the Gloamin'', and 'Keep Right on to the End of the Road' world famous, died on *20 February* aged 79.

'Lia-fàil', or the 'Stone of Destiny' originally Scotland's Coronation Stone, was stolen from Westminster Abbey on *15 December*. The stone was taken by Scottish Nationalists and its disappearance sparked off a nationwide hunt. The police received a telephone call on *13 April* the following year, that the Stone of Destiny was in Arbroath Abbey (where, coincidentally, the first Declaration of Independence was written in 1320). Making an immediate search, the police found it. However, Nationalists claim it was a fake and that the original stone is in a church in Dundee.

1957

Glasgow Rangers suffered their worst defeat at Hampden Park on *19 October*. Their chief rivals, Celtic, beat them 7–1 in the League Cup final. The last goal of the match was a penalty against Rangers, taken by Celtic's Willie Fernie. Rangers' unfortunate goalie was George Niven.

1958

Aberdeen-born Denis Law became the youngest footballer to play for Scotland when he played in his first international against Wales at Cardiff on *8 October*. He was 18 years and seven months of age.

The first work on the construction of the Forth Road Bridge began on *21 November*. It was to be the longest suspension bridge in Europe.

1959

Scotland's first nuclear power station, Chapelcross, was opened on *2 May*.

1961

The 6156-foot-long Forth Road Bridge was opened by Her Majesty the Queen on *4 September*, linking Edinburgh by a main road, later a motorway, to the northern cities.

1963

The Earl of Home became Britain's Prime Minister on *18 October*, and renounced his peerage to become Sir Alec Douglas-Home. The Queen appointed him on the previous PM's advice and after consulting with Sir Winston Churchill and other elder statesmen. The deputy premier, Rab Butler, was expected to get the job as he was the favourite among the Conservative MPs. Some even claimed that a 'magic circle' supervised by Harold Macmillan, who was Prime Minister at that time, cooked up a plot to keep him out.

There has never been such a frenetic leadership struggle in the Tory party before or since. Much of it had to do with who was chosen for the PM's job, as Lord Home was most certainly not liked by his fellow MPs. Both Iain Macleod, Leader of the Commons, and Enoch Powell, the Minister of Health, refused to serve under him. Apparently the Scottish peer was not much liked by the electorate either. They voted him out of office almost a year to the day later. He was Britain's shortest-serving Prime Minister.

1964

A band of the King's African Rifles played 'A Scottish Soldier' at midnight on *6 July*, as Nyasaland became the independent state of Malawi. The music was played as a reminder of the days spent in Edinburgh by Malawi's first president, Dr Banda, who studied there and where he was also an elder of the Church of Scotland.

1966

On Wednesday, *18 August* the Tay Road Bridge was opened by the Queen Mother. Thousands turned up to see the event. The bridge, connecting Dundee to Newport in Fife, was built by William Logan, a local contractor, at a cost of £5 million.

1967

Glasgow Celtic, the Scottish League Champions – who won every trophy in every Scottish cup tournament they entered that year – became the first British football team to win the European Cup. They beat the Italian champions Inter Milan 2–1 in Lisbon, Portugal on *25 May*. The Celtic team who played that day have since been nicknamed 'the Lisbon Lions'.

The Scottish National Party won their first seat in a by-election at the end of the year when Mrs Winnie

Ewing took Hamilton from Labour. In the local elections the following year they took 100 seats.

The British liner the *QEII*, or the *Queen Elizabeth II* was launched at Clydebank on *20 September*.

1971

The worst disaster at a Scottish football match happened at Rangers' home ground stadium on *2 January*. After an 'old firm' match with Celtic an ugly accident occurred when a barrier collapsed and 66 people were crushed to death.

1972

There was a terrible tragedy in Glasgow on Friday *25 August* when seven firemen were killed in a fire. They were trying to extinguish the blaze at a cash-and-carry warehouse in Kilbirnie Street near Eglington Toll when a roof fell in, killing all of the seven men.

It was a particularly bad day for the city. Four boys aged between eight and eleven were drowned when they fell from a raft into the Forth and Clyde Canal in the city's Clydebank district.

1974

This was the best year in the history of the Scottish National Party. There were two general elections that year and in the first, in *February*, they won seven seats and in *October* they won eleven, the greatest number they have ever held.

1975

The first oil was pumped ashore from the North Sea pipelines to Aberdeen on *11 June*. The oil was pumped from Aberdeen, through the pipeline. The oil tap that released the flow was turned on by Her Majesty the Queen.

1976

Monifieth businessman Mr Tom Docherty (42) broke the British distance record for gliding on Saturday *24 July*. He left the Scottish Gliding Union field at Portmoak, Scotlandwell, around midday to arrive at

Ford airfield in Bognor Regis in Sussex at 7 pm. Mr Docherty, who had been gliding for 26 years, made the trip in a glass-fibre Kestrel 19-metre sail plane.

Dundee's abattoir was called the world's worst slaughterhouse at a meeting of the National Union of Farmers at Forfar on *3 August*. Mr Charles Young, one of the main speakers, after hearing of complaints to the police regarding the building, told his audience, 'I suggest you support the police all you can . . . otherwise the abattoir will become a byword or a legend in bad planning.' Mr Young added, 'It is the most futile effort in planning I ever knew.'

Scotsman David Wilkie won a Gold Medal for Britain in the 200 metres breast stroke and a Silver for the 100 metres breast stroke at the Montreal Olympic Games on Saturday *7 August*. It gave Britain her first men's swimming gold. On the same day, having achieved his greatest goal, Wilkie announced his retirement from swimming.

1988

A terrorist bomb exploded in a Boeing 747 flying from Frankfurt to New York on Wednesday, *21 December* causing the plane to crash into the Dumfriesshire country town of Lockerbie. The plane demolished some houses in the area and wreckage was strewn in the nearby countryside. Two hundred and seventy people were killed in this worst of terrorist atrocities to strike Scotland.